Symbol Signs

The System of
Passenger/Pedestrian Oriented Symbols
Developed for the
U.S. Department of Transportation

The American Institute
of Graphic Arts

Visual Communication Books
Hastings House, Publishers
New York 10016

The 50 passenger/pedestrian Symbol Signs
illustrated in this volume are free of copyright.

SYMBOL SIGNS REPRO ART

The AIGA has published a portfolio, SYMBOL SIGNS
REPRO ART, which makes available reproduction art of
the complete set of 50 passenger/pedestrian symbols
developed for the U.S. Department of Transportation.
Each symbol is printed on 9″ x 11″ Kromekote cover stock.
A 24-page booklet of guidelines describing how the
symbols are to be used and standardized red and green paint
chips for sign manufacture are also included.

$40 AIGA members; $50 nonmembers

To order the portfolio, please contact:
The American Institute of Graphic Arts
1059 Third Avenue · New York, N.Y. 10021
(212) 752-0813

Second Printing, December 1982.
Prepared by The American Institute of Graphic Arts
1059 Third Avenue, New York 10021
for the Office of Facilitation, Assistant Secretary for Environment,
Safety, and Consumer Affairs, United States Department of Transportation.

Library of Congress Cataloging in Publication Data

Symbol signs.

   (Visual communication books)
   Bibliography: p.
   1. Transportation markings.   2. Traffic signs and
signals.   I. American Institute of Graphic Arts.
II. United States.   Dept. of Transportation.   III. Series.
TA1245.S95   625.7′94   81-7102
ISBN 0-8038-6777-8   AACR2

Published simultaneously in Canada by
Saunders of Toronto, Ltd., Markham, Ontario.

Printed in the United States of America.

Contents

The American Institute of Graphic Arts is a national, non-profit organization, founded in 1914, which conducts an interrelated program of competitions, exhibitions, publications, educational activities, and projects in the public interest to promote the advancement of graphic design.

Members of the Institute are involved in the design and production of books, magazines, and periodicals, as well as corporate, environmental, and promotional graphics. Their contribution of specialized skills and expertise provides the foundation for the Institute's program. Through the Institute, members form an effective, informal network of professional assistance that is a resource to the profession and to the public.

Caroline Hightower
Executive Director

David Brown
President

The Committee is an advisory committee sponsored by the Department of Transportation, Assistant Secretary for Environment, Safety and Consumer Affairs, and coordinated by the Office of Facilitation. Its major objectives are to develop a comprehensive system of transportation-related symbols to serve U.S. domestic and international transport needs. The membership is comprised of representatives principally from Federal agencies, transportation-oriented industries and associations and other qualified sources outside Government. The Committee's functions are solely advisory and its recommendations are forwarded to the Secretary of Transportation for his approval.

Mr. William R. Myers
Executive Director
U.S. Department of Transportation

Mr. Thomas H. Geismar
Chairman
American Institute of Graphic Arts

Mr. Robert J. Bengtsson
AMTRAK

Mr. Michael Carrasco, Jr.
U.S. Department of Interior

Mr. Robert E. Conner
U.S. Department of Transportation/FHWA

Mr. John J. Corbett
Airport Operators Council International

Mr. Gene Cox
U.S. Department of Transportation/FRA

Mr. Robert F. Crecco
U.S. Department of Transportation

Mr. Ralph J. Haller

Mr. Stanley Hamilton
National Association of Motor Bus Owners

Mr. Richard G. Huber
U.S. Department of Interior

Mr. J. Stuart Jamison
U.S. Department of Transportation/FAA

Mr. Colson E. Jones
Pennsylvania Transportation Commission

Mr. Harold Lewis Malt
Industrial Designers Society of America

Mr. Patrick J. McCue
Association of American Railroads

Mr. Lee E. Metcalfe
U.S. Department of Transportation

Mr. James P. Moceri

Mr. Edmond C. Neumann
U.S. Department of Agriculture

Mr. Robert E. Redding
U.S. Department of Transportation

Mr. Warren G. Stambaugh
American Automobile Association

Mr. C. Langhorne Washburn
U.S. Department of Commerce/USTS

Mr. James A. Wilding
U.S. Department of Transportation/FAA

Thomas H. Geismar is a partner in the firms, Chermayeff and Geismar Associates, graphic and exhibition designers in New York, and Cambridge Seven Associates, architects in Cambridge, Massachusetts. He has designed trademarks and symbols for numerous major U.S. companies and other institutions and government agencies. He has also been involved in numerous sign programs, among them the design of new signs and graphics for the Metropolitan Boston Transportation Authority, air terminals in New York, South Carolina and Oklahoma, and signage and symbols for the National Park Service. He is a Vice President of the AIGA and chairman of the AIGA Signs and Symbols Committee.

Seymour Chwast is the co-founder and partner in the well known Push Pin Studios. Among his clients are Olivetti, Pan American World Airways, The Xerox Corporation, IBM, CBS, and the Metropolitan Museum of Art for which he has designed a guidebook and map. He has written and illustrayed numerous childrens' books and has wide experience in conveying ideas and meanings through illustrations. Several of his posters are in the permanent collection of the Museum of Modern Art. He is a Vice President of the AIGA

Rudolph deHarak is a well known graphic, industrial, and exhibit designer, as well as an experienced teacher. He has developed symbols and trademarks for a number of corporations, and organized a major exhibition on international trademarks for the AIGA. He is currently designing several signage systems, including graphics, signing and mural projects for Flushing Bus Terminal; Harlem River State Park; Lower Main Steet Mall, Paterson, New Jersey; and others. He was formerly a Director of the AIGA.

John Lees is a partner in the firm Herman and Lees Associates of Cambridge, Massachusetts. He has designed signage and identity programs for clients in Europe, Africa, and Asia as well as the U.S.,including the master plan for the road signs of Sardinia, along with the signing and commercial graphics for the Costa Smeralda Resort, and signing programs for the Central Housing Board of India, the Aga Kahn Hospital and Medical College of Pakistan and Polaroid. The firm also acted as graphic consultants on a number of studies, including the Bolt, Barank and Newman Study for the Federal Highway Administration; a master plan for the State University of New York; and the Federally sponsored 'Signs and Lights' study for the city of Boston.

Massimo Vignelli who is head of Vignelli Associates is highly experienced in signing projects, having designed the graphic standards for the Metropolitan Washington and New York Subway Systems. He is also responsible for the New York City Subway maps. His identification and signing programs include buildings for the City College of New York, Harvard University, First National Citibank Corporation, and a theatre, college and museum complex for the Minneapolis Society of the Fine Arts Park. Along with his wife, an architect, he won the AIA Industrial Arts Medal in 1973. Examples of his graphic and product design are in the Museum of Modern Art's permanent collection. He is a Director of the AIGA.

Cook and Shanosky Associates These designers have worked on a wide variety of projects during 12 years as partners. Much of their work has concentrated in the area of corporate identity, symbols, trademarks, and logotypes. The firm has received national and international recognition in major exhibitions around the world. Their work has appeared in the Whitney Museum in addition to a number of graphic arts publications.

Page, Arbitrio, and Resen Ltd. The firm has a great deal of experience with signage projects of all types. They have created vehicular and pedestrian control signage for the National Airlines Terminal at JFK International Airport. In addition, they are preparing signage for South Terminal at Logan International Airport in Boston, Sky Harbor International Airport in Phoenix, and Collins Place in Sydney, Australia.

Don Moyer and Karen Moyer served jointly as Project Coordinators for the Symbol Sign project. Their responsibilities included completion of the inventory of existing symbols and design and production of the Symbol Sign Report.

Mark Ackley and **Juanita Dugdale** served as Project Coordinators for the Symbol Sign project. Their responsibilities included completion of the inventory of existing symbols and design and production of the Symbol Sign Report.

The Yale University Department of Computer Science and Professor Alvin Eisenman of Yale University's Graphic Design Department were extremely helpful with technical problems during the project and their cooperation is greatly appreciated.

Throughout all the studies, William R. Myers, Director of the Office of Facilitation of the U.S. Department of Transportation, was not only a knowledgeable and determined client, but also a constant source of encouragement. It is only through his efforts that this project happened.

Over the past several years, numerous international, national and local organizations have developed sets of symbols for use in facilitating passenger and pedestrian orientation in transportation-related facilities and at the sites of large international events. (Throughout this book the term 'symbol' is used to denote both true symbols such as the Red Cross, and pictorial devices, pictographs, or pictograms, which are illustrative in nature.)

Some of these groups have attempted to establish international standards, but have been criticized for the overall graphic quality of the drawings, as well as for some of the concepts. Others, especially those associated with temporary events such as Olympic Games or World's Fairs, have spent considerable effort to achieve graphic excellence. At the same time, they have made a conscious effort to give their symbols a unique graphic character inappropriate for wider functional needs.

Out of all this effort have come a number of well-conceived and well-executed individual symbols, but no one complete system that seems immediately adaptable to the needs of transportation-related facilities.

To develop such a system, and to take full advantage of the work done to date by others throughout the world, the American Institute of Graphic Arts in cooperation with the U.S. Department of Transportation, Office of Facilitation, compiled an inventory of symbol systems which have actually been used in transportation-related facilities or large international events.

Two reports were produced. The first published in 1974 recommended the adoption and public use of a basic group of 34 transportation-related passenger and pedestrian oriented symbol signs. The second was published in 1979 and not only added sixteen additional messages but also provided an expanded series of standards for the form and shape in which the symbol signs can be used. This book is a compilation of the two reports.

The added messages were determined on the basis of actual experience with the initial group of symbol signs. For the most part the new group represents messages that the operators or administrators of various facilities found missing from the first study. Some of the ones included are of lesser importance, but others, such as Cashier, Escalator and Litter Disposal, could have extensive use beyond the needs of transportation-related facilities.

The most significant, and most controversial symbol is the one proposed for Exit. Here we are suggesting a major change in the way that fire exits are marked. Much time was spent dealing with this particular message, and a special section of the Guidelines explains the rationale behind this recommendation.

The added standards for the form and shape in which the symbol signs can be used are also a result of actual experience with the initial group. We were told by a number of designers that, for one reason or another, the use of the square shape and/or a light color background under certain conditions caused problems which in effect prevented them from using the symbol signs at all. While the AIGA Committee still recommends the original form as the standard, we felt it was appropriate to also allow a limited number of other forms in order to assure that the symbol signs do get used. To clearly define the acceptable alternatives, we have described each, and shown how it would affect the entire combined group of symbol signs.

To undertake the project, the AIGA appointed a committee of five members with considerable experience and interest in the problem. It was determined that the task of the committee would be to review the major symbol systems in use around the world, to analyze the effectiveness of each based on personal experience, and from this analysis to develop a clear concept for each message area. The committee's next task was to determine who should draw the symbols and prepare the guidelines for using them. Finally they were to direct the execution of this work by other AIGA members.

The committee was composed of Thomas H. Geismar (chairman), Seymour Chwast, Rudolph deHarak, John Lees, and Massimo Vignelli.

Briefly, the work proceeded in the following manner. First a list of initial message areas was developed by D.O.T. and its Advisory Committee on Transportation-Related Signs and Symbols along with the AIGA committee.

Concurrently, we set to work to gather together examples, manuals, and research from around the world, and to organize this material into the selected list of message areas so that each could be properly evaluated. Once that had been done by the AIGA, project coordinators, Don Moyer and Karen Moyer, Juanita Dugdale, and Mark Ackley, it became the task of the committee to evaluate the inventory of existing symbols and to recommend the best approach to take for each message area. In doing so, every effort was made to find satisfactory symbols among the existing systems.

As described more fully later in this book, each existing symbol was analyzed independently by each committee member. In addition, each message group was discussed at some length by the whole committee, and the recommendations were arrived at as a joint decision of the group. Some decisions were easily made; others provoked considerable discussion.

These decisions were then submitted to a working panel of the D.O.T. Advisory Committee for review. That panel thoroughly reviewed the recommendations, and made a determination on each, accepting many, revising some, and rejecting a few. The AIGA then reviewed the working panel's response, and reviewed some of its recommendations. All questions were resolved as outlined in this book.

In evaluating the existing material, it was always presumed that all recommended symbol concepts would require at least some graphic modifications or refinements to be incorporated into a uniform graphic system. Other symbols required new or modified concepts and consequently considerable original drawing.

For these modifications, the committee determined that the firm of Cook and Shanosky Associates was best qualified, and they were given a contract by the AIGA to design all the symbols in a uniform graphic style, following the committee's basic recommendations. During an intensive period of work, Roger Cook and Don Shanosky developed the specified designs, and for each message area periodically submitted sketches and alternative designs for review. The committee members all took an active role in reviewing the work in progress, and in a series of meetings attempted to resolve with the designers the problem of reducing some rather complex images to their most basic and expressive components. When the design for each message area was finally agreed upon, Cook and Shanosky prepared finished artwork.

To undertake the development of a set of guidelines for using the symbols and relating them to the verbal messages, the committee chose the firm of Page, Arbitrio and Resen. Based on some basic determinations made by the committee, this firm prepared alternative examples of the kinds of signs that would result from the establishment of certain guidelines concerning lettering size and style, the use of colors and directional arrows, etc. These suggested guidelines can be found in a separate section of the book.

The intent of these guidelines is not to provide a rigid set of rules, but rather a suggested range of possibilities within which the problems most commonly encountered in facility signage can be resolved without sacrificing the integrity of the symbol system.

Finally, in the course of this project we have found common agreement on a few key points concerning symbols:

We are convinced the effectiveness of symbols is strictly limited. They are most effective when they represent a service or concession that can be represented by an object, such as a bus or bar glass. They are much less effective when used to represent a process or activity such as Ticket Purchase, because these are complex interactions that vary considerably from mode to mode and even from carrier to carrier.

We are convinced that symbols are useless at a facility unless incorporated as part of an intelligent total sign system. The use of symbols alone, without consideration for the verbal messages and all other signing, will only add to the confusion.

We are convinced that it is more harmful to oversign than to undersign. To mix messages about relatively insignificant activities and concessions with essential public messages weakens the communication. While there may be some messages beyond this basic group that require symbols, only those messages that are truly essential should be considered.

Having said this, we do feel that, properly used, symbols can play an important role in facilitating communication and orientation in transportation-related facilities. We also believe that a well conceived and well designed set of symbols can win wide acceptance. Hopefully this book brings that a step closer to reality.

Thomas H. Geismar
Chairman
Committee on Signs and Symbols
The American Institute of Graphic Arts

1

Inventory

Considerable time, effort and expense has been expended by various groups throughout the world for the development of pictorial symbols. By analyzing the results of these efforts, the AIGA Signs and Symbols Committee sought to find acceptable solutions among these existing symbols.

The first task was to develop a group of initial message areas. For this, the Department of Transportation Office of Facilitation, and the AIGA Committee formed the following list, divided into four categories.

Public Services contains messages which represent services widely used in transportation-related facilities.

Concessions includes messages that are related to commercial activities.

Processing Activities includes messages that represent important passenger-related procedures.

Regulations represents messages announcing mandatory procedures.

In this listing we have attempted to describe the message areas with wording that corresponds to conventional terms, without over simplifying. These are not necessarily the words that would appear on actual signs. The guideline section of this report offers recommendations about the suggested wording that should appear with the symbols.

Public Services

Telephone
Mail
Currency Exchange
Cashier
First Aid
Lost and Found
Coat Check
Baggage Lockers
Escalator Up
Escalator Down
Stairs Up
Stairs Down
Elevator
Toilets, Men
Toilets, Women
Toilets
Nursery
Drinking Fountain
Waiting Room
Information
Hotel Information
Air Transportation
Heliport
Taxi
Bus
Ground Transportation
Rail Transportation
Water Transportation

Concessions

Car Rental
Restaurant
Coffee Shop
Bar

Shops
Barber Shop/Beauty Salon
Barber Shop
Beauty Salon

Processing Activities

Ticket Purchase
Baggage Check-in
Baggage Claim
Customs
Immigration
Departing Flights
Arriving Flights

Regulations

Smoking
No Smoking
Parking
No Parking
No Dogs
No Entry
Exit
Fire Extinguisher
Litter Disposal

After the list of messages was established, the project concentrated on making an inventory of the existing symbols that correspond to those messages. Drawings were collected from 24 separate sources including symbols developed for use at transportation facilities such as international airports and railway networks, as well as international events such as Olympic Games and World Expositions.

Although the committee was familiar with many theoretical and experimental systems these designs were avoided in the inventory in favor of symbols developed for use in actual situations.

The purpose of the inventory was to discover where strong symbol concepts already existed and where further efforts needed to be concentrated, in order to produce more satisfactory concepts.

The pertinent symbols collected from each of the 28 sources are displayed in the Appendix to allow study of characteristics that function within the source group but may not be evident by looking at any symbol alone.

Throughout the inventory and evaluation the symbols are identified by initials derived from the name of the sources. These abbreviations and notes about the sources are provided in the following list.

ADCA
Australian Department of Civil Aviation
1972
Australia
Designed by Kinneir, Calvert, and Associates.
These symbols were developed as part of an extensive signage program for use at Australian airport facilities.

ADV
German Airports Association
Arbeitsgemeinschaft Deutscher
Verhehrsflughafen
1968
Germany
Designed by M. Krampen and H. W. Kapitzki.
These symbols were designed to be used by the airports in the Republic of Germany and the Federal Republic of Austria. They were created as part of an extensive signing program.

ATA
Air Transport Association
1966
United States
Designed by Arnold Thompson Associates.
These symbols were proposed for use at international airports.

BAA
British Airports Authority
1972
England
Designed by Kinneir, Calvert, and Tuhill.
These symbols were developed as part of an extensive signage program for British airports. They are currently being used at several sites including Heathrow Airport.

CSS
Canadian National Signing System
Canada
Designed by Hunter Straker Templeton Ltd.
for use in a national bilingual signing program.

D/FW
Dallas-Fort Worth International Airport
1973
United States
Designed by Henry Dreyfuss Associates.
These symbols were developed for use at the Dallas-Fort Worth International Airport. They are similar to the symbols the Dreyfuss office developed for American Airlines.

FA
Frankfurt Airport
Federal Republic of Germany
Designed by Otl Eicher and staff; these symbols were originally developed for use at the Munich Olympic Games.

IATA
International Air Transport Association
1966
Canada
These symbols were developed for use at international airport facilities.

ICAO
International Civil Aviation Organization
1970
Canada
These symbols were proposed for use at international airport facilities.

KFAI
KFAI AB
Sweden
Designed by Claes Tottie.
Symbols for Kooperative Fobundet, Sektor D.

LVA
Las Vegas Airport
1972
United States
Designed by Richard Graef and John Follis.
These symbols were developed for use at the McCarren International Airport at Las Vegas, Nevada.

MM
Mexico City Metro
1969
Mexico
Designed by Lance Wyman.
These symbols were developed as part of a sign system for the Mexico Metro.

NPS
National Park Service
1970
United States
Designed by Chermayeff and Geismar Associates.
These symbols were developed as part of an extensive signage program for use in the United States' National Parks. The symbols are currently being installed in park facilities throughout the country.

NRR
Netherlands Railroads
Nederlandse Spoorwegen
Netherlands
These symbols are used extensively in the country's railway facilities.

O'64
Tokyo Olympic Games
1964
Japan
Design directed by Masaru Katzumie.
These symbols were created for use at the public facilities of the International Olympic Games.

O'68
Mexico Olympic Games
1968
Mexico
Designed by Lance Wyman and Beatrice Cole.
These symbols were created for use at the public facilities of the International Olympic Games.

O'72
Munich Olympic Games
1972
Federal Republic of Germany
Designed by Otl Aicher and Staff.
These symbols were created for use at the public facilities of the International Olympic Games. They are used extensively at Frankfurt International Airport.

O'76
Montreal Olympic Games
1976
Canada
Designed by Georges Huel and Pierre-Yves Pelletier.
In order to guide athletes and spectators through facilities, these symbols were designed for the summer Olympic Games.

Pg
Picto 'grafics
1972
United States
Designed by Paul Arthur and Associates.
These symbols are from a large assortment of drawings that are available commercially as fabricated signs.

Port
Port Authority of New York and New Jersey
1971
United States
Designed by Owen Scott, Supervisor of design staff of the Aviation Department.
These symbols were created for use at Port Authority transportation facilities and are being used at JFK International Airport.

SP
Swedish National Parks
Statens Naturvardsverk
1972
Sweden
These symbols were developed as part of signage program for the parks of Sweden.

S/TA
Seattle-Tacoma Airport
1971
United States
Designed by Donald J. Gerands and Richardson Associates.
These symbols were developed as part of a signage program for the Seattle-Tacoma International Airport. In addition to their use there, they are being installed in the airport at Guam.

TA
Tokyo Airport
1970
Japan
Designed by Aisaku Murakoshi.
These symbols were developed for use at the Tokyo Narita International Airport.

TC
Transport Canada, Air
Ministry of Air Transportation
1974
Designed by the design staff of the Ministry of Air Transportation for use in Canadian airport facilities.

UIC
International Union of Railways
Union International Chemin de Fer
1965
International Organization
These symbols were proposed for use at international railway facilities. Many are being used in European railway facilities.

WO'72
Sapporo Winter Olympics
1972
Japan
Designed by Fukuda Shigeo.
These symbols were created for use at the public
facilities of the International Winter Olympic
Games.

X'67
Montreal Expo
1967
Canada
Designed by Paul Arthur and Associates.
These symbols were created for use at the public
facilities of the international exposition.

X'70
Osaka Expo
1970
Japan
Designed by Eknan Kenji, GK Industrial Design
Institute, Isozaki Arata, and Fukuda Shigeo.
These symbols were created for use at the public
facilities of the international exposition.

Analysis / Evaluation

Within each message area, the inventory organized all the symbols into groups. All the symbols in a group are based on the same fundamental concept. Although it is not always possible to make entirely satisfactory decisions about which characteristics justify creation of a new group and which are insignificant, it was clear that for most messages, well defined symbol concepts exist. These groups and the statements intended to summarize them are included on the inventory and evaluation pages. Neither the order of the concept groups nor the order of the symbols within each group were intended to indicate preferences or judgments about their strengths and weaknesses.

Evaluations were made in two ways. Using the inventory pages as a guide, each Committee member was given a symbol concept evaluation sheet which enabled him to privately rate every individual symbol in the collection without discussion with other Committee members. Using a scale of 1 to 5, with 1 representing weakness and 5 representing strength, each symbol was rated on its semantic, syntactic, and pragmatic dimensions. The averages of these ratings are displayed on the Evaluation Chart pages under the headings Semantic, Syntactic, and Pragmatic.

In addition, the Committee as a whole evaluated the symbol concepts. This was done through discussions which concentrated on rating the relative strength of each symbol concept as grouped on the evaluation pages. These ratings are displayed on the Evaluation Chart pages under the column marked Group.

All of these ratings are of course subjective. However, they are based on many years of personal and professional experience by five individuals with varied interests and backgrounds.

Symbol Concept Evaluation Sheet

This is an example of the ballots used by the individual AIGA Committee members to evaluate all of the symbols collected in the Inventory.

```
              AIGA
              Transportation
              Sign and Symbol
              Project


 name


 message       ARRIVING FLIGHTS


       source     semantic    syntactic   pragmatic
 1     ADV        1 2 3 4 5   1 2 3 4 5   1 2 3 4 5
 2     ICAO       1 2 3 4 5   1 2 3 4 5   1 2 3 4 5
 3     O'72       1 2 3 4 5   1 2 3 4 5   1 2 3 4 5
 4     PG         1 2 3 4 5   1 2 3 4 5   1 2 3 4 5
 5     TA         1 2 3 4 5   1 2 3 4 5   1 2 3 4 5
 6     TC         1 2 3 4 5   1 2 3 4 5   1 2 3 4 5
 7     D/FW       1 2 3 4 5   1 2 3 4 5   1 2 3 4 5
 8     PORT       1 2 3 4 5   1 2 3 4 5   1 2 3 4 5
 9     ATA        1 2 3 4 5   1 2 3 4 5   1 2 3 4 5
 10    FA         1 2 3 4 5   1 2 3 4 5   1 2 3 4 5
 11               1 2 3 4 5   1 2 3 4 5   1 2 3 4 5
 12               1 2 3 4 5   1 2 3 4 5   1 2 3 4 5
 13               1 2 3 4 5   1 2 3 4 5   1 2 3 4 5
 14               1 2 3 4 5   1 2 3 4 5   1 2 3 4 5
 15               1 2 3 4 5   1 2 3 4 5   1 2 3 4 5
```

Frequently the words legibility, readability, and clarity enter discussions about symbols. While these words reflect realistic concerns, they are too inaccurate to be useful in evaluating symbols. To produce consistent judgments a more objective basis was needed. Three very fundamental aspects served as the outline for the committee's evaluations.

All visual communication, including symbols, have three distinct dimensions; semantic, syntactic, and pragmatic. The strengths and weaknesses of every symbol can be evaluated in relation to these basics of communication.

The **semantic** dimension refers to the relationship of a visual image to a meaning.
How well does this symbol represent the message?
Do people fail to understand the message that the symbol denotes?
Do people from various cultures misunderstand this symbol?
Do people of various ages fail to understand this symbol?
Is it difficult to learn this symbol?
Has this symbol already been widely accepted?
Does this symbol contain elements that are unrelated to the message?

The **syntactic** dimension refers to the relationship of one visual image to another.
How does this symbol look?
How well do the parts of this symbol relate to each other?
How well does this symbol relate to other symbols?
Is the construction of this symbol consistent in its use of figure/ground, solid/outline, overlapping, transparency, orientation, format, scale, color and texture?
Does this symbol use a hierarchy of recognition?
Are the most important elements recognized first?
Does this symbol seriously contradict existing standards or conventions?
Is this symbol, and its elements, capable of systematic application for a variety of interrelated concepts?

The **pragmatic** dimension refers to the relationship of a visual image to a user.
Can a person see the sign?
Is this symbol seriously affected by poor lighting conditions, oblique viewing angles, and other visual 'noise'?
Does this symbol remain visible throughout the range of typical viewing distances?
Is this symbol especially vulnerable to vandalism?
Is this symbol difficult to reproduce?
Can this symbol be enlarged and reduced successfully?

In actuality, these three dimensions are interrelated in complex ways. Nevertheless, recognizing them makes it possible to logically isolate and evaluate specific qualities.

The AIGA Committee's intent, throughout this project, was to take full advantage of work done to-date, to build on existing systems, to discover and assimilate strong concepts where they existed and concentrate on developing original designs only where no existing symbol was adequate.

It was always understood that each symbol would require at least some redrawing to give a common visual language to the system. The column headed Recommendations on the Evaluation Chart page reflects the AIGA committee's brief that was given to the designers following the evaluation and subsequent discussions.

Frequently the recommendations propose experimentation with alternative solutions. This is necessary because the symbols are visual elements and in the final analysis it is necessary to see the alternatives to judge them.

The recommendations do not necessarily correspond exactly to the judgments expressed in the evaluations. An essential consideration in the development of the symbols must be how they will relate to each other. The strict numerical ratings of existing symbols make no provision for this requirement.

Finally, in the course of the design and related discussions further ideas developed which were incorporated in the final drawings. It is because of this that the final symbol designs created do not necessarily correspond exactly to the committee's original recommendations.

Symbol Sources

Throughout this report the symbol sources are identified using the abbreviations shown in this list.

ADCA	Australian Department of Civil Aviation
ADV	German Airports Association
ATA	Air Transport Association
BAA	British Airports Authority
CSS	Canadian National Signing System
D/FW	Dallas-Fort Worth International Airport
FA	Frankfurt Airport
IATA	International Air Transport Association
ICAO	International Civil Aviation Organization
KFAI	KFAI AB, Sweden
LVA	Las Vegas Airport
MM	Mexico City Metro
NPS	National Park Service
NRR	Netherlands Railroads
O'64	Olympic Games, Tokyo 1964
O'68	Olympic Games, Mexico 1968
O'72	Olympic Games, Munich 1972
O'76	Olympic Games, Montreal 1976
Pg	Picto'grafics
Port	Port Authority of New York and New Jersey
SP	Swedish National Parks
S/TA	Seattle-Tacoma Airport
TA	Tokyo Airport
TC	Transport Canada, Air
UIC	International Union of Railroads
WO'72	Winter Olympic Games, Sapporo 1972
X'67	Expo 67, Montreal
X'70	Expo 70, Osaka

Telephone

1

X'67	 O'72	 ATA	 UIC	 BAA
 S/TA	 IATA	 SP	 WO'72	 D/FW
 X'70	 Pg	 NPS	 KFAI	 NRR
 TA	 Port	 TC	 ICAO	 ADV

2

O'68

3

O'64

4

ADCA

Concept Description	Symbol Source	Evaluation				Symbol Design Recommendations
		Semantic	Syntactic	Pragmatic	Group	
1 **Telephone handset.**	X'67	5	3	3	**5**	This message presents a dilemma for the committee. The inventory clearly shows that the telephone handset is widely used around the world. But it is an awkward shape, one that might be confused with other symbols, such as the wrench used in highway signs to represent repairs.
	O'72	5	3	3		
	ATA	5	4	4		
	UIC	5	4	4		
	BAA	5	3	4		
	S/TA	5	3	4		
	IATA	5	3	3		
	SP	5	2	3		
	WO'72	4	2	2		
	D/FW	4	2	2		
	X'70	5	2	3		
	Pg	5	2	3		
	NPS	5	3	3		
	KFAI	4	2	2		
	NRR	5	2	2		
	TA	5	3	3		
	Port	5	3	3		
	TC	5	3	3		
	ICAO	5	2	3		
	ADV	5	3	3		

To the committee, both the telephone dial, O'64, and the front view of the telephone, O'68, are clearer representations of a phone. The problem is that they represent obsolete telephone styles.

While it is not our intention to develop new symbols where another has already been well established, we believe that the symbol used for telephone is one of the easiest to establish because the instrument is so universally used and known. Therefore, we advise that in addition to developing a satisfactory drawing of a handset, there should be experiments with a front view of an up-to-date phone.

We feel that none of the drawings of the handsets are completely satisfactory. The object should not be over simplified and abstracted, as for example the X'70 version. It should also not be merely a photographic depiction, like the ICAO version.

The committee feels that it makes little difference whether the image is placed vertically or at an angle. That decision should involve an evaluation of the relationships between this drawing and the others in the initial group.

Summary:
Modify drawing of Group 1 concept; experiment with front view of modern telephone.

Concept Description	Symbol Source	Evaluation				Symbol Design Recommendations
2 **Telephone dial.**	O'68	5	5	5	**5**	
3 **Front view of dial telephone.**	O'64	5	5	4	**5**	
4 **Handset and dial.**	ADAC	3	2	2	**3**	

Mail

1

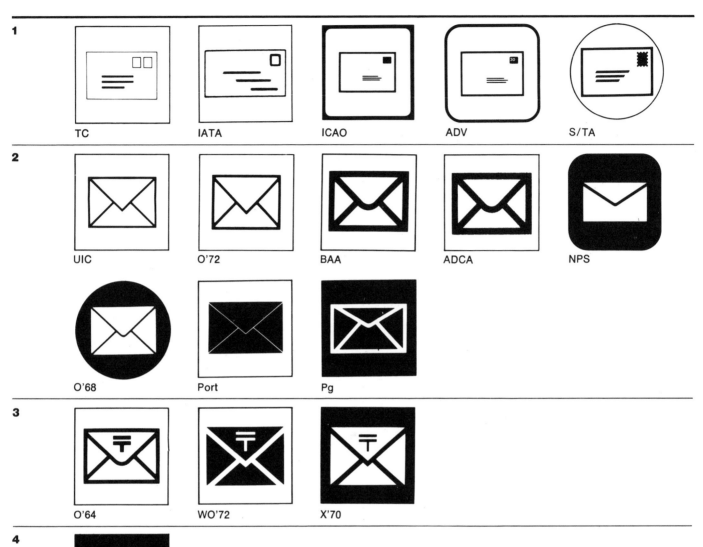

TC

IATA

ICAO

ADV

S/TA

2

UIC

O'72

BAA

ADCA

NPS

O'68

Port

Pg

3

O'64

WO'72

X'70

4

KFAI

SP

Concept Description	Symbol Source	Evaluation				Symbol Design Recommendations
		Semantic	Syntactic	Pragmatic	Group	
1 **Front view of envelope.**	TC	4	2	3	**5**	Although a front view of an envelope is a strong representation of Mail, the committee is convinced that it is unusually difficult to create a strong drawing of an envelope that includes a stamp and address.
	IATA	4	2	3		
	ICAO	4	2	3		
	ADV	4	2	3		
	S/TA	4	2	3		
2 **Side view of envelope.**	UIC	5	4	4	**5**	Fortunately, the back of an envelope is also a satisfactory representation of postal services. We believe that drawings such as the O'72 or UIC symbols show a good starting point. In addition, a rounded flap on the envelope may be included to aid understanding.
	O'72	5	4	4		
	BAA	5	4	4		
	ADCA	5	4	4		
	NPS	4	2	3		
	O'68	5	4	3		
	Port	4	3	3		
	Pg	4	3	3		
3 **Backview of envelope with postal symbol.**	O'64	4	3	3	**4**	
	WO'72	4	3	3		
	X'70	4	3	3		
4 **Back view of envelope, dropping through slot.**	KFAI	3	3	3	**4**	
	SP	4	3	3		

We believe that the envelope should be white. Dark envelopes are confusing because they contradict the convention of white or light colored envelopes.

Summary:
Modify Group 2 concept.

Currency Exchange

1

BAA

UIC

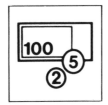

IATA

ATA

ADV

ADCA

O'72

NRR

TA

2

D/FW

ICAO

3

TC

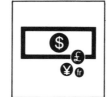

Port ✱

4

Pg

5

O'68

6

WO'72

X'70

Concept Description	Symbol Source	Evaluation				Symbol Design Recommendations
		Semantic	Syntactic	Pragmatic	Group	
1 **Paper money and coins, with numbers.**	BAA	2	3	2	**4**	Several drawings in the inventory attempt to represent Currency Exchange with an assortment of paper money and coins. Of those shown in Groups 1 and 2, we judge the Port version to be the strongest because of its emphasis on currency symbols instead of numbers. All these drawings are highly complex images. Therefore, we recommend that an attempt be made to redraw this concept in a bolder way.
	UIC	3	3	2		
	IATA	3	2	2		
	ATA	3	2	2	
	ADV	3	2	2	
	ADCA	2	2	2	
	O'72	2	2	2	
	NRR	3	2	2	
	TA	3	2	2	
2 **Paper money and coins.**	D/FW	3	2	2	**2**	At the same time, in a search for a more simplified concept, we recommend that consideration be given to combining the dollar sign with two or three other currency symbols. This idea is similar to the concept represented in Group 4, except that the symbols could each be contained in a circle to suggest coins as well as maintain seperation between the symbol and adjacent typographic elements.
	ICAO	3	2	2		
3 **Paper money and coins, with currency symbols.**	TC	3	2	3	**4**	**Summary:** **Modify drawing of Port symbol in Group 2. Also experiment with modified drawing of Group 4 concept.**
	Port	3	2	2		
4 **Money symbols.**	Pg	4	4	4	**3**	
5 **Dollar sign.**	O'68	4	5	5	**5**	
6 **Symbol for Japanese Yen, ¥.**	WO'72	4	5	5	**5**	
	X'70	4	5	5		

Cashier

1

CSS

2

O'72

Concept Description	Symbol Source	Evaluation				Symbol Design Recommendations
		Semantic	Syntactic	Pragmatic	Group	
1 **Figure next to silhouette of cash register**	CSS	3	3	3	**3**	An obvious approach for the message Cashier is to simply show a cash register. However, it will be difficult to draw effectively because the familiar cash register design is rapidly becoming obsolete, as are the familiar raised tabs with numerals. Some experimental drawings based on this concept (essentially the CSS symbol, with and without the figure) should be undertaken.
2 **Portion of cash register**	O'72	1	2	2	**1**	Presuming the validity of our above stated concerns, however, we recommend that a new symbol concept be established for this message. Since a person looking for the cashier is looking for the place to make a monetary transaction, the dollar sign itself would be an appropriate and understandable concept, especially within the context of a shop, customs area, etc., where it would be used. To make the mark obviously a symbol, and consistent with the group, we recommend that the dollar sign be placed within an outline circle, as was done with the question mark for the information symbol.

(This same concept could easily be adopted by other nations, substituting the symbol of their own monetary system for the dollar sign.)

Summary:
Use dollar sign within a circle as in Information symbol previously adopted.

First Aid

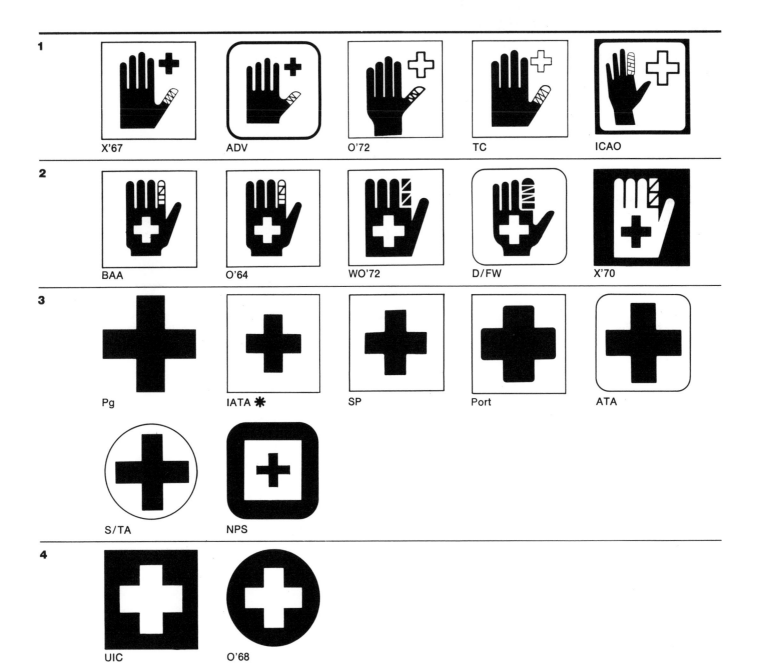

1
X'67 ADV O'72 TC ICAO

2
BAA O'64 WO'72 D/FW X'70

3
Pg IATA ✳ SP Port ATA

S/TA NPS

4
UIC O'68

Concept Description	Symbol Source	Semantic	Syntactic	Pragmatic	Group	Symbol Design Recommendations
1 **Hand with bandaged finger or thumb, including cross symbol nearby.**	X'67 ADV O'72 TC ICAO	3 3 3 3 3	3 2 2 3 2	3 3 2 2 2	**4**	As shown in the third group, the cross is an extremely bold symbol that is widely recognized and accepted. We recommend that it alone should be used to represent First Aid. We propose this even though we are aware that other symbols are used in parts of the Middle East, (Moslem countries use the Red Crescent; Israel uses the Red Star of David; and Iran uses the Red Lion).
2 **Hand with bandaged finger, cross symbol superimposed over hand.**	BAA O'64 WO'72 D/FW X'70	3 3 3 3 3	3 3 3 2 3	3 3 3 3 3	**4**	In our judgment this symbol should consistently be red because this color is strongly associated with this message. Even the First Aid symbols listed above retain the color red. The green cross, which we have considered, represents Pharmacy in parts of Europe and sometimes Safety in the United States. Neither are appropriate for First Aid.
3 **Cross symbol alone, dark cross on light background.**	Pg IATA SP Port ATA S/TA NPS	4 5 5 5 4 4 4	4 5 5 3 3 3 3	4 5 5 4 4 4 3	**5**	We believe the IATA symbol in Group 3 is well proportioned. However, the final drawing should be evaluated in relation to the other symbols in the initial group. We feel that, in those symbols that use an upraised hand with bandaged finger, in Groups 1 and 2, the cross is the element that communicates most effectively. It can obviously work more strongly if it is used alone. **Summary:** **Adopt Group 3 concept of red cross on white background.**
4 **Cross symbol alone, light cross on dark background.**	UIC O'68	3 3	3 3	4 4	**2**	

Lost and Found

1

X'67

S/TA

Pg

X'70

2

O'72

TC

D/FW

ICAO

ADV

NRR

3

ATA

UIC

IATA

Concept Description	Symbol Source	Semantic	Syntactic	Pragmatic	Group	Symbol Design Recommendations
1 **Suitcase and question mark.**	X'67 S/TA Pg X'70	4 4 4	3 3 4	3 3 4	**4**	This is a difficult idea to express in a symbol. Of the concepts shown in the inventory, we accept the idea of combining a question mark with items that are typically lost. We believe that inquiries about lost baggage are usually made directly to the carrier involved. Therefore the Group 1 concept, though simpler and better drawn than most of the others, is inappropriate to the idea of Lost and Found as a place where personal items are collected.
2 **Assorted items; umbrellas, gloves and question mark.**	O'72 TC D/FW ICAO ADV NRR	3 2 2 2 2 3	2 2 2 2 2 2	3 2 3 2 2 2	**4**	We recommend that the Group 2 concept be adopted, but be redrawn in a simpler and bolder manner than the existing symbols. An umbrella and glove, probably the most frequently lost items, should be combined with a question mark. Unlike the question mark proposed for the message 'Information', this one need not be enclosed inside a circle. **Summary:** **Adopt Group 2 concept, combining umbrella, glove, and question mark.**
3 **Assorted items with tags attached.**	ATA UIC IATA	2 2 2	2 2 3	3 2 3	**2**	

Coat Check

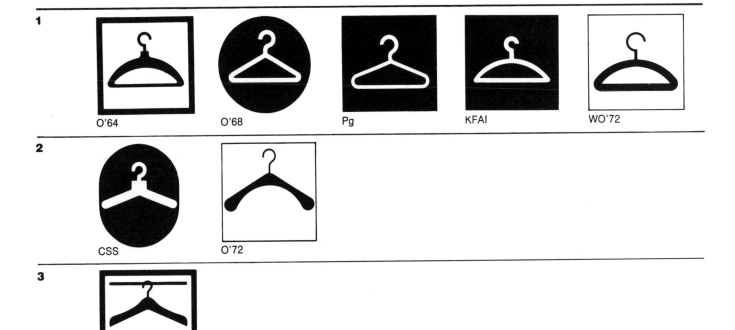

1

O'64 O'68 Pg KFAI WO'72

2

CSS O'72

3

X'67

Concept Description	Symbol Source	Evaluation				Symbol Design Recommendations
		Semantic	Syntactic	Pragmatic	Group	
1 **Coat hanger with bottom bar**	O'68	4	4	4	**5**	The Committee agrees that a coat hanger is the best symbol for Coat Check.
	Pg	4	4	4		
	KFAI	4	2	3		The coat hanger which includes the bottom bar, as in Group 1, is the most successful representation. Of these we prefer the O'68 and Pg versions. But we recommend that the hook face to the right (as in the KFAI version) so as to avoid confusion with a question mark.
	WO'72	4	3	3		
	O'64	4	2	2		
2 **Coat hanger without bottom bar**	CSS	4	2	3	**4**	
	O'72	4	2	3		**Summary:** **Adopt Group 1 concept.**
3 **Coat hanger on bar**	X'67	4	2	3	**3**	

Baggage Lockers

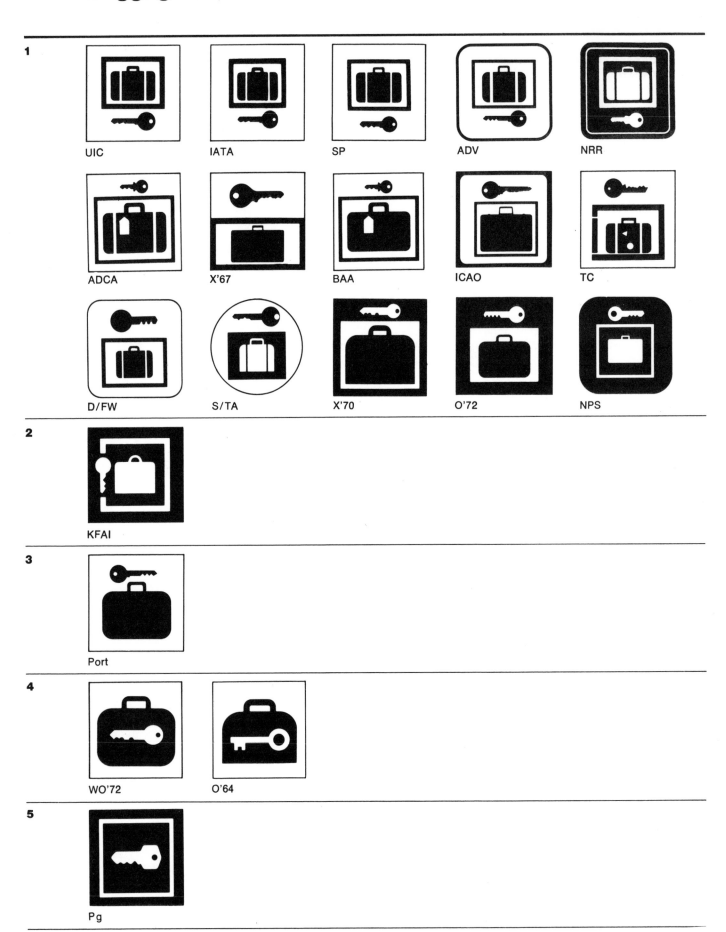

1

UIC   IATA   SP   ADV   NRR

ADCA   X'67   BAA   ICAO   TC

D/FW   S/TA   X'70   O'72   NPS

2

KFAI

3

Port

4

WO'72   O'64

5

Pg

Concept Description	Symbol Source	Evaluation				Symbol Design Recommendations
		Semantic	Syntactic	Pragmatic	Group	
1 **Suitcase inside box, key nearby.**	UIC	4	4	4	**4**	The concept of a suitcase inside a box, with a key above the box, as shown in the first group, is a strong and widely used representation of the message Baggage Lockers. We recommend that this idea be adopted.
	IATA	4	4	4		
	SP	4	4	4		
	ADV	4	3	4		A standard representation of a suitcase should be established and consistently used in drawings showing luggage, including Baggage Lockers, Baggage Check-in, and Baggage Claim.
	NRR	4	3	3		
	ADAC	4	3	4		
	X'67	4	2	2		The committee feels that a suitcase alone, such as that used in the X'67 or Port versions, presents a potential readability problem. We believe that the suitcase drawing should include some distinctive details, such as straps, stickers, or tags. Vertical straps are the most commonly used by the drawings in the inventory and are preferred.
	BAA	4	4	4		
	ICAO	4	2	3		
	TC	4	4	4		
	D/FW	4	3	4		
	S/TA	4	2	3		
	X'70	4	3	3		For the locker, we recommend using a reasonably bold box, like the locker in the UIC symbol. To avoid looking like a frame, the box may need some characteristic to suggest the locker's door. The broken line in the TC symbol attempts this. We recommend further experimentation with this idea.
	O'72	4	3	4		
	NPS	4	3	4		
2 **Suitcase inside box, key on one side of box.**	KFAI	4	3	3	**2**	**Summary:** **Adopt Group 1 concept, with key above box containing suitcase. Experiment with method of drawing box as a locker.**
3 **Suitcase and key.**	Port	3	4	4	**2**	
4 **Key inside suitcase.**	WO'72	3	4	4	**3**	
	O'64	3	3	3		
5 **Key inside box.**	Pg	2	3	3	**1**	

Escalator Up

1

FA   O'72

2

TC

3

KFAI   X'70

4

Pg

5

D/FW

Concept Description	Symbol Source	Evaluation				Symbol Design Recommendations
		Semantic	Syntactic	Pragmatic	Group	
1 **Figure about to step off escalator at top**	FA O'72	3 3	3 3	3 3	**3**	We recommend that the escalator be of outline form, as in the KFAI symbol. However, we recommend experimentation with indicating a floor transition at the top and the bottom (as in the TC and D/FW symbols). We prefer a neutral direction figure as in KFAI and X'70.
2 **Figure ascending escalator with floor transitions**	TC	2	2	2	**2**	When an arrow is needed to delineate escalator movement, it should be added outside the escalator form. (Although direction of escalator movement can be delineated this way, it may be preferable at times to combine a general Escalator symbol, without an arrow, with a separate directional arrow panel, when for example it is necessary to point the way to the Escalators.)
3 **Neutral direction figure on escalator with arrow inside**	KFAI X'70	3 4	4 3	4 3	**4**	**Summary:** **Adopt Group 3 concept, but show floor transitions at top and bottom. When an arrow is necessary, bring it outside of escalator form.**
4 **Escalator with stair profile and arrow outside**	Pg	2	2	2	**2**	
5 **Escalator with stair profile and arrow at top floor transition**	D/FW	2	2	2	**2**	

Escalator Down

1

FA

O'72

2

TC

3

KFAI

4

Pg

5

D/FW

Concept Description	Symbol Source	Evaluation				Symbol Design Recommendations
		Semantic	Syntactic	Pragmatic	Group	
1 **Figure about to step off escalator at bottom**	FA O'72	3 3	3 3	3 3	**3**	We recommend that the same symbol described under "Escalator Up" be used. An arrow to delineate direction of escalator movement should be added outside the escalator form where the more appropriate general symbol can be combined with a separate directional arrow panel.
2 **Figure descending escalator with floor transitions**	TC	3	2	2	**2**	**Summary:** **Adopt Group 3 concept, but show floor transitions at top and bottom. When an arrow is necessary, bring it outside of escalator form.**
3 **Neutral direction figure on escalator with arrow inside**	KFAI	3	4	3	**4**	
4 **Escalator with stair profile and arrow outside**	Pg	2	2	2	**2**	
5 **Escalator with stair profile and arrow at bottom floor transition**	D/FW	2	2	2	**2**	

Stairs Up

1

MM   O'76   O'72   TC

2

Pg

3

X'70

4

D/FW   UIC

5

CSS   KFAI

Concept Description	Symbol Source	Evaluation				Symbol Design Recommendations
		Semantic	Syntactic	Pragmatic	Group	
1 **Profile of figure ascending stairs**	MM O'76 O'72 TC	4 4 4 4	2 2 2 2	3 3 3 2	**4**	Since the same stairs can be used to go either up or down, and since at an entrance to a stairway there is usually a choice of up or down, the Committee recommends that a single symbol be developed for the general concept "stairs" rather than separate symbols for "Stairs Up" and "Stairs Down."
2 **Stair profile**	Pg	3	2	2	**2**	We recommend basic adoption of the KFAI design (Group 5) but without the arrow for general use. Where it is necessary to indicate direction, an arrow could be added, or a separate arrow panel combined with the general "stairs" symbol.
3 **Figure on stair profile with arrow inside**	X'70	2	2	2	**2**	**Summary:** **Adopt KFAI concept, but without arrow for general application.**
4 **Stair profile with arrow at top floor transition**	D/FW UIC	2 2	2 2	2 2	**2**	
5 **Stair profile with arrow outside**	CSS KFAI	3 4	2 3	3 4	**4**	

Stairs Down

1

 MM
 O'76
 O'72 
 TC 

2

 D/FW
 UIC

3

 CSS
 KFAI

Concept Description	Symbol Source	Evaluation				Symbol Design Recommendations
		Semantic	Syntactic	Pragmatic	Group	
1 **Profile of figure descending stairs**	MM	4	2	3	**4**	See recommendation for Stairs-Up.
	O'76	4	2	3		
	O'72	4	3	3		**Summary:**
	TC	4	2	2		**Use same symbol as developed for Stairs-Up.**
2 **Stair profile with arrow at bottom floor transition**	D/FW	2	2	2	**2**	
	UIC	2	2	2		
3 **Stair profile with arrow outside**	CSS	3	2	3	**4**	
	KFAI	3	4	3		

Elevator

1

S/TA

D/FW

ATA

Pg

2

KFAI ✳

3

TC

ICAO

ADV

O'72

BAA

4

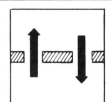

IATA

5

ADCA

Concept Description	Symbol Source	Evaluation				Symbol Design Recommendations
		Semantic	Syntactic	Pragmatic	Group	
1 **Figure(s) inside a box, arrow above pointing up and arrow below pointing down.**	S/TA	3	2	2	**4**	The committee believes that a box with figures inside and arrows pointing up and down is the best approach for this symbol.
	D/FW	3	3	3		
	ATA	3	3	3		We feel that the KFAI symbol in Group 2, showing a group of three figures inside a box, is especially well drawn. The scale of the figures in relation to the outline of the box is more successful than the other drawings.
	Pg	3	3	3		
2 **Figures inside a box, arrows above pointing up and down.**	KFAI	4	3	3	**4**	Although there should be some experimentation with alternative positions for the arrows, they should probably remain on top of the box because there they suggest cables.
3 **Figures inside a box, cable attached and shaft indicated.**	TC	3	2	2	**4**	**Summary: Adopt Group 2 concept.**
	ICAO	3	2	2		
	ADV	3	2	2		
	O'72	2	3	2		
	BAA	3	2	2		
4 **Two arrows, each pointing through opening in a horizontal band.**	IATA	1	2	2	**1**	
5 **Vertical arrow pointing both up and down, positioned between vertical bars.**	ADCA	2	4	3	**1**	

Toilets, Men

1

WO'72 ✳

SP

Port

ICAO

O'72

ADV

O'64

KFAI

X'70

NPS

O'68

TA

2

BAA

UIC

IATA

ATA

D/FW

ADCA

S/TA

NRR

Pg

3

X'67

Concept Description	Symbol Source	Evaluation				Symbol Design Recommendations
		Semantic	Syntactic	Pragmatic	Group	
1 **Standing man, legs together.**	WO'72	5	4	3	**3**	The inventory clearly shows that a standing male figure is the conventional representation of toilet facilities for men.
	SP	5	2	3		
	Port	5	4	4		
	ICAO	4	2	3		Research has disclosed that figures with legs separated, such as those in Group 2, are inviting targets for graffiti artists, especially when the background color is light. Therefore, the committee recommends beginning with a drawing similar to the bold figure used in the O'72 symbol. We encourage experimenting with a narrow vertical line to separate the legs, such as the X'70 drawing. We also are interested in experimenting with rounding the ends of the legs (the feet) to soften the form.
	O'72	5	3	4		
	ADV	3	2	3		
	O'64					
	KFAI	4	2	3		
	X'70	5	4	4		
	NPS	5	3	3		
	O'68	5	3	3		
	TA	3	1	2		

Summary:
Adopt Group 1 concept, using basic WO'72 drawing with more delination of limbs.

Concept Description	Symbol Source	Evaluation				Symbol Design Recommendations
2 **Standing man, legs apart.**	BAA	4	2	3	**3**	
	UIC	4	3	3		
	IATA	4	3	3		
	ATA	4	3	3		
	D/FW	4	3	3		
	ADCA	4	3	3		
	S/TA	4	3	3		
	NRR	4	2	3		
	Pg	4	2	3		

Concept Description	Symbol Source	Evaluation				Symbol Design Recommendations
3 **Standing man, inside box.**	X'67	4	3	3	**2**	

Toilets, Women

1

WO'72

Port

ICAO

X'70

O'68

BAA

ADCA

O'64

SP

O'72

TA

2

UIC

IATA

ATA

D/FW

ADV

S/TA

NPS

NRR

KFAI

Pg

3

X'67

Concept Description	Symbol Source	Evaluation				Symbol Design Recommendations
		Semantic	Syntactic	Pragmatic	Group	
1 **Standing woman, arms close to figure.**	WO'72	3	2	3	**3**	The inventory clearly shows that a standing female figure is the conventional representation of toilet facilities for women.
	Port	3	3	3		
	ICAO	3	2	2		In our judgment, this symbol should be based on the kind of figure used in the second group of drawings, especially the IATA and ATA versions.
	X'70	4	2	2		
	O'68	3	2	2		
	BAA	3	2	3		
	ADCA	4	2	3		The head of the figure should be detached and the body may need to be reproportioned to better relate to the drawing of the male figure.
	O'64					
	SP	3	2	3		
	O'72	3	2	3		
	TA	3	2	3		

Summary:
Adopt Group 2 concept, adjusting drawing to conform with the male figure.

Concept Description	Symbol Source	Evaluation				Symbol Design Recommendations
2 **Standing woman, arms extended.**	UIC	4	3	3	**3**	
	IATA	4	3	3		
	ATA	4	3	4		
	D/FW	4	4	4		
	ADV	4	2	4		
	S/TA	3	2	3		
	NPS	4	3	3		
	NRR	3	3	3		
	KFAI	4	3	3		
	Pg	3	2	3		

Concept Description	Symbol Source	Evaluation				Symbol Design Recommendations
3 **Standing woman, inside box.**	X'67	4	2	2	**2**	

Toilets

1

BAA

UIC

SP

KFAI

NRR

2

D/FW

TC

ICAO

3

O'64

ADV

Port

TA

Concept Description	Symbol Source	Evaluation				Symbol Design Recommendations
		Semantic	Syntactic	Pragmatic	Group	
1 **WC**	BAA	1	3	3	**5**	We recommend that the symbol concept of two standing figures, a man and a woman, as shown in the second and third groups, be accepted.
	UIC	1	3	3		
	SP	1	2	3		The same figures created for men's toilets and women's toilets should be utilized here.
	KFAI	1	3	3		
	NRR	1	3	3		
2 **Standing man and woman separated by vertical line.**	D/FW	4	3	4	**4**	We suggest experimenting with a line to separate the figures, but caution against overcomplicating the drawing.
	TC	4	3	4		Although the WC (water closet) concept is widely accepted in Europe, it is not familiar in the United States.
	ICAO	3	2	3		
3 **Standing man and woman.**	O'64	3	3	3	**2**	**Summary:** **Adopt Group 2 concept, using standing figures developed for men's and women's toilets.**
	ADV	3	3	3		
	Port	4	2	3		
	TA	4	2	3		

Nursery

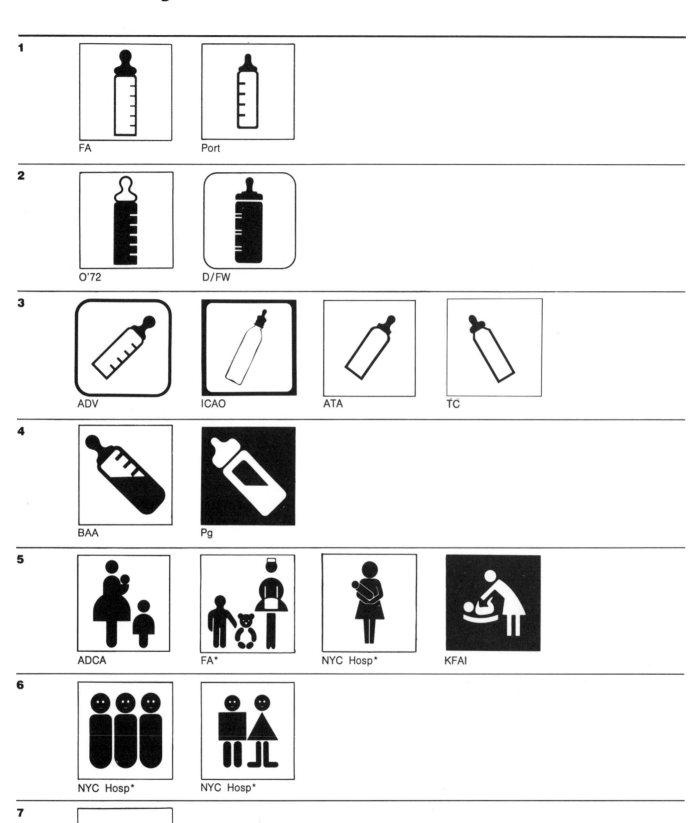

1
FA
Port

2
O'72
D/FW

3
ADV
ICAO
ATA
TC

4
BAA
Pg

5
ADCA
FA*
NYC Hosp*
KFAI

6
NYC Hosp*
NYC Hosp*

7
O'72

*Related category or system

Concept Description	Symbol Source	Evaluation				Symbol Design Recommendations
		Semantic	Syntactic	Pragmatic	Group	
1 **Upright baby bottle, dark outline**	FA Port	3 3	3 3	3 3	**3**	The Committee feels that a baby bottle (Groups 1, 2, 3, & 4) is a good, well established concept to use. The figures of mother and child (e.g. ADCA), or female diapering infant (KFAI) are more illustrative and less strong as symbols. Yet, we are aware that there is considerable opposition from certain segments of the U.S. population to the idea of bottle feeding.
2 **Upright baby bottle, dark solid**	O'72 D/FW	2 2	2 2	2 2	**2**	In view of this, we recommend development of a new symbol that simply shows an infant. This is essentially an adaptation of the Group 6 concept, except that there should only be one figure, and it should be clearly an infant, and less cartoon-like in style.
3 **Tilting baby bottle, dark outline**	ADV ICAO ATA TC	3 3 4 3	3 2 3 3	3 2 3 3	**4**	
4 **Tilting baby bottle with formula**	BAA Pg	3 3	3 2	3 2	**3**	
5 **Grouping of mother or nurse with infants**	ADCA FA* NYCH* KFAI	3	3	3	**3**	
6 **Infants**	NYCH* NYCH*					
7 **Teddy bear**	O'72					

Summary:
Adopt Group 6 concept of showing figure, but use only single figure of infant.

Drinking Fountain

1

BAA

ICAO

UIC

CSS

O'68

2

KFAI

3

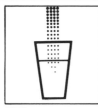
O'72

O'76

SP

4

NPS

5

O'64

Pg

Concept Description	Symbol Source	Evaluation				Symbol Design Recommendations
		Semantic	Syntactic	Pragmatic	Group	
1 **Tap and glass**	BAA ICAO UIC CSS O'68	2 2 2 2 2	2 2 2 2 2	2 2 2 2 3	**2**	The concepts of tap and glass, or glass and water (Groups 1, 2, 3, & 4) are inappropriate for the concept "Drinking Fountain" in the United States even though they may be appropriate for the message "Drinking Water." The two symbols shown in Group 5 are appropriate to the message "Drinking Fountain", but the disembodied head is too mysterious.
2 **Water pouring from tap into glass**	KFAI	2	2	2	**2**	The Committee believes that the message is best conveyed by showing a figure drinking at a fountain. Lacking any existing symbols that can be easily adapted, we recommend that a new design be developed.
3 **Water pouring into glass**	O'72 O'76 SP	2 2 2	2 2 2	2 2 2	**2**	**Summary:** **Develop new design showing figure drinking from a U.S. style water fountain.**
4 **Glass filled with water**	NPS	2	2	2	**2**	
5 **Head and water spout**	O'64 Pg	3 3	2 2	2 2	**3**	

Waiting Room

1

NRR UIC

2

FA O'72

3

Pg

4

ATA

Concept Description	Symbol Source	Evaluation				Symbol Design Recommendations
		Semantic	Syntactic	Pragmatic	Group	
1 **Seated figure with clock and suitcase**	NRR UIC	3 3	2 2	2 2	**3**	The Committee believes that a seated figure or figures, with a clock, is the best approach for this message. We prefer the simplicity of the FA and O'72 designs (Group 2) but feel the seat should be more clearly expressed. We recommend experimentation with both two figures (male and female) in a back-to-back configuration, and with a single seated figure.
2 **Seated figures, back-to-back, with clock**	FA O'72	3 3	3 3	3 3	**4**	**Summary:** **Adopt Group 2 concept, using either single or back-to-back figures.**
3 **Seated figure**	Pg	2	2	2	**2**	
4 **Clock and seat**	ATA	3	2	3	**3**	

Information

1

Port

O'68

2

D/FW

ATA

IATA

Pg

NPS

BAA ✻

ADCA ✻

S/TA

TA

X'70

3

O'72

KFAI

NRR

TC

UIC

SP

5

ADV

ICAO

6

WO'72

O'64

Concept Description	Symbol Source	Evaluation				Symbol Design Recommendations
		Semantic	Syntactic	Pragmatic	Group	
1 **Pair of question marks.**	Port	3	3	3	**3**	There have been no really good symbols developed to convey this message. The question mark as a symbol for Information is not completely satisfactory, but it has the potential of becoming effective and it is being widely used.
	O'68	3	4	3		
2 **Question mark.**	D/FW	4	3	3	**2**	We recommend that the question mark be used, but we feel that something more is needed to make it obvious that it is a symbol and to avoid confusion with adjacent typography.
	ATA	4	3	4		
	IATA	3	2	3		One obvious choice is to enclose the question mark in a shape, such as the circle used in the BAA symbol.
	Pg	3	3	3		
	NPS	3	3	3		
	BAA	4	4	5		**Summary:** **Adopt Group 2 concept, with question mark inside a circle as in the BAA pictogram.**
	ADCA	4	4	5		
	S/TA	3	3	3		
	TA	3	3	3		
	X'70	3	2	3		
3 **Question mark and lower case i.**	O'72	2	2	2	**3**	
4 **Lower case i.**	KFAI	2	3	3	**2**	
	NRR	2	2	2		
	TC	2	2	3		
	UIC	2	2	3		
	SP	2	2	3		
5 **Seated figure with standing figure, and question mark.**	ADV	2	1	2	**1**	
	ICAO	2	1	2		
6 **Fists pointing in various directions.**	WO'72	1	2	2	**1**	
	O'64	1	2	1		

Hotel Information

1

ICAO

2

TC

D/FW

3

IATA

4

O'72

5

NPS

Pg

6

SP

Concept Description	Symbol Source	Evaluation				Symbol Design Recommendations
		Semantic	Syntactic	Pragmatic	Group	
1 **Telephone, building shape, and the word Hotel.**	ICAO	2	2	2	**2**	This message is not adequately expressed by any of the existing drawings. None of the building shapes suggest a structure the size or scale of a hotel, the telephone that is included in several is not necessarily appropriate, and the bed is a symbol that is very difficult to render well.
2 **Telephone, building shape, and bed.**	TC D/FW	2 2	2 2	2 2	**2**	**Summary:** **Experiment with the standard Information symbol combined with elements to express Hotel.**
3 **Building shape and bed.**	IATA	2	2	3	**2**	
4 **Figure in bed, and telephone.**	O'72	3	3	3	**3**	
5 **Figure in bed.**	NPS Pg	3 3	3 3	3 3	**3**	
6 **Bed, perspective view.**	SP	3	4	3	**2**	

Air Transportation

1

LVA   Pg ✳   NPS   ADV ✳   O'72

UIC   NRR

2

DOT

Concept Description	Symbol Source	Evaluation				Symbol Design Recommendations
		Semantic	Syntactic	Pragmatic	Group	
1 **Plan view of airplane.**	LVA	4	3	4	**5**	We believe that the message, Air Transportation, is well represented by a plan view of an airplane. The inventory shows that this is a well established symbol concept.
	Pg	5	5	5		
	NPS	4	3	4		
	ADV	5	4	5		The committee recommends that a bold and simple drawing, such as the Pg or ADV symbols, be accepted.
	O'72	5	4	5		
	UIC	5	3	5		
	NRR	4	3	3		Details or characteristics that tend to define a specific type of aircraft should be avoided because they cannot remain up to date. Instead the drawing should be a symbol for airplanes in general.
						We encourage consideration of the airplane's orientation (left, right, and up) to reinforce directional information.
2 **Picture of 747.**	DOT	3	3	3	**3**	**Summary:** **Adopt concept of simplified plan view of airplane. Modify ADV or Pg drawings.**

Heliport

1

SP

O'72 ✳

D/FW

ADV

ICAO

Concept Description	Symbol Source	Evaluation				Symbol Design Recommendations
		Semantic	Syntactic	Pragmatic	Group	
1 **Side view of helicopter.**	SP	5	4	5	**5**	The committee recommends a side view of a helicopter to represent this message.
	O'72	5	4	5		
	D/FW	5	4	5		A symbol with the bold qualities of the other drawings in the initial grouup is needed.
	ADV	5	4	5		
	ICAO	4	2	2		

We feel that the O'72 symbol is a good starting point. We suggest replacing its wheels with a horizontal bar to represent the familiar landing pontoons.

Summary:
Adopt concept of using side view of helicopter. Modify O'72 drawing using pontoons.

Taxi

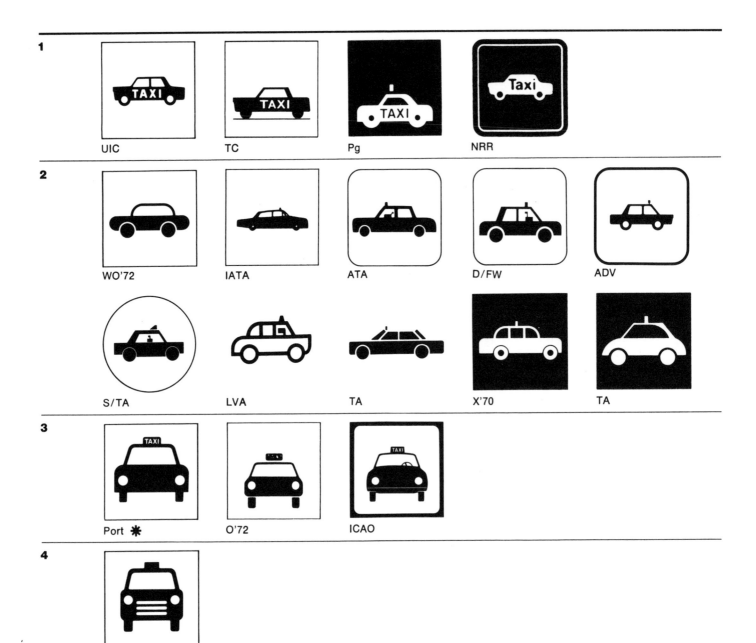

1
UIC   TC   Pg   NRR

2
WO'72   IATA   ATA   D/FW   ADV

S/TA   LVA   TA   X'70   TA

3
Port ✳   O'72   ICAO

4
BAA

Concept Description	Symbol Source	Evaluation				Symbol Design Recommendations
		Semantic	Syntactic	Pragmatic	Group	
1 **Side view of taxi with the word Taxi.**	UIC TC Pg NRR	4 4 4 4	3 3 3 2	3 3 4 3	**5**	In our judgment a front view of a taxi is slightly clearer than a side view because the distinctive taxi lamp on top of the car is clearly visible. A standard representation of an automobile should be established and used for this message, as well as for Car Rental.
2 **Side view of taxi.**	WO'72 IATA ATA D/FW ADV S/TA LVA TA X'70 TA	3 3 4 4 4 4 4 4 4 4	3 1 3 3 3 2 3 2 3 3	2 2 3 3 2 3 3 2 3 3	**5**	The drawing should avoid too much detail and any characteristics that tend to define a specific car model should be eliminated. Of the examples found in the inventory, we believe that the Port symbol is well proportioned and bold. The taxi lamp should be defined as clearly and boldly as possible but without any lettering. **Summary:** **Adopt Group 4 concept, but with drawing similar to the Port version, without the word Taxi.**
3 **Front view of taxi with the word Taxi.**	Port O'72 ICAO	5 5 4	5 4 3	5 5 4	**5**	
4 **Front view of taxi.**	BAA	5	5	5	**5**	

Bus

1

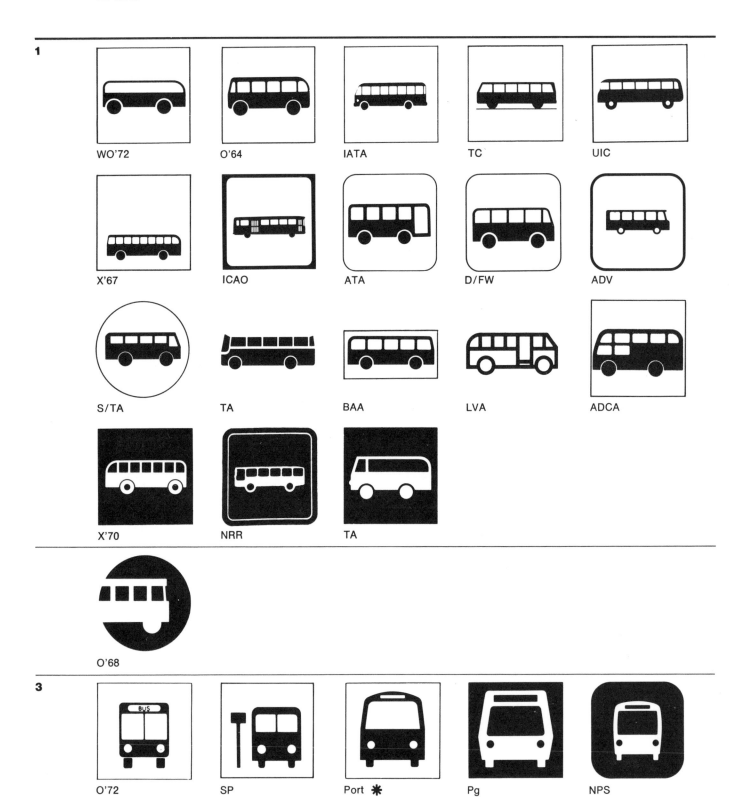

WO'72

O'64

IATA

TC

UIC

X'67

ICAO

ATA

D/FW

ADV

S/TA

TA

BAA

LVA

ADCA

X'70

NRR

TA

2

O'68

3

O'72

SP

Port ✳

Pg

NPS

Concept Description	Symbol Source	Evaluation				Symbol Design Recommendations
		Semantic	Syntactic	Pragmatic	Group	
1 **Side view of bus.**	WO'72	4	2	3	**5**	Both front and side views are relatively clear representations of the idea of bus transportation. Since the front view is clear and fits well into the square format, we recommend its adoption.
	O'64	4	4	4		
	IATA	4	2	3		
	TC	4	3	4		
	UIC	4	3	3		The drawing should avoid too much detail. It should represent buses in general and avoid any characteristics that tend to define a specific model of bus.
	X'67	4	3	4		
	ICAO	4	2	2		
	ATA	5	4	4		
	D/FW	5	4	4		Of the examples shown in the third group, we prefer the Port version because it is well proportioned to represent a standard commercial bus, while remaining simple and bold.
	ADV	4	2	3		
	S/TA	4	4	4		
	TA	4	4	3		
	BAA	4	4	4		
	LVA	4	4	3		**Summary:**
	ADCA	4	4	4		**Adopt Group 3 concept, modifying Port Authority drawing.**
	X'70	4	3	3		
	NRR	4	3	3		
	TA	4	3	3		
2 **Side view of portion of bus.**	O'68	3	2	2	**2**	
3 **Front view of bus.**	O'72	5	4	4	**5**	
	SP	4	3	4		
	Port	5	4	5		
	Pg	4	3	4		
	NPS	4	3	3		

Ground Transportation

1

D/FW

Concept Description	Symbol Source	Evaluation				Symbol Design Recommendations
		Semantic	Syntactic	Pragmatic	Group	
1 **Side view of bus and taxi.**	D/FW	5	4	4	**5**	The Dallas-Fort Worth system is the only one in the inventory that has a symbol to represent Ground Transportation. Nevertheless, we believe that combining representations of these two different transportation modes in a single symbol is an acceptable concept for use where space is limited. Otherwise a number of appropriate individual drawings could be used side by side (e.g. Bus, Taxi, Rail, etc.). The combined drawings should utilize the standard symbols developed for Bus and Taxi, keeping them in proper scale to each other in a side by side relationship. Recommendations for drawing these vehicles can be found under Bus and Taxi. **Summary:** **Adopt D/FW concept, using standard Bus and Taxi drawings in a side-by-side relationship.**

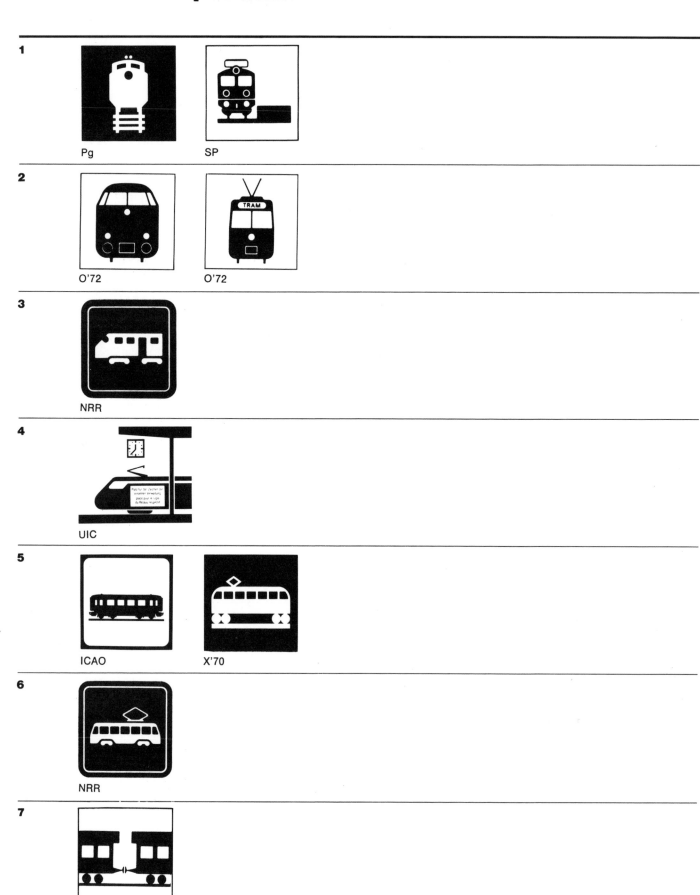

1 Pg   SP

2 O'72   O'72

3 NRR

4 UIC

5 ICAO   X'70

6 NRR

7 IATA

Concept Description	Symbol Source	Evaluation				Symbol Design Recommendations
		Semantic	Syntactic	Pragmatic	Group	
1 **Front view of train, including track or ground.**	Pg	5	4	3	**4**	We feel that a front view of a train is the strongest drawing concept to represent Rail Transportation.
	SP	4	3	3		
2 **Front view of train.**	O'72	5	4	4	**4**	Of the examples collected, we find the Pg drawing closest to the look of an American train. We recommend experimental drawings both with and without tracks. The railroad tracks in the Pg drawing resemble a ladder. Perhaps they would be more effective if shown in perspective.
	O'72	4	3	3		
3 **Side view of train.**	NRR	4	3	3	**4**	
4 **Side view of locomotive including platform.**	UIC	3	2	2	**3**	
5 **Side view of train car including track or ground.**	ICAO	4	2	3	**4**	
	X'70	4	3	3		
6 **Side view of train car.**	NRR	4	3	3	**4**	
7 **Train cars coupled.**	IATA	2	1	2	**2**	

The drawing should be simple and bold in the style of the other symbols in the initial group but with enough details to distinguish it from a bus.

Summary:
Adopt concept of front view of train. Experiment with drawings that include tracks or platform.

Water Transportation

1

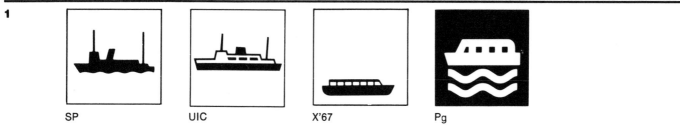

SP   UIC   X'67   Pg

2

O'72 ✳

Concept Description	Symbol Source	Evaluation				Symbol Design Recommendations
		Semantic	Syntactic	Pragmatic	Group	
1 **Side view of ship.**	SP	4	2	3	**4**	The committee anticipates that this symbol will be used primarily as a trailblazer and that it should be a representation of an ocean-going cruise ship.
	UIC	4	3	3		
	X'67	3	3	3		
	Pg	4	3	3		A side view of a ship, such as the UIC symbol in Group 1, can be satisfactory. But we feel that it is difficult for this kind of of drawing to suggest the large scale of a cruise ship.
2 **Front view of ship.**	O'72	5	4	4	**4**	Therefore, we favor a front view, such as the O'72 drawing. To avoid looking too much like a freighter, the drawing must be reproportioned so that it is tall, extending high above the water. The water too must be redrawn because in the O'72 version it resembles an open book.

Summary:
Adopt Group 2 concept, adjusting drawing to clearly portray large cruise ship in water.

Car Rental

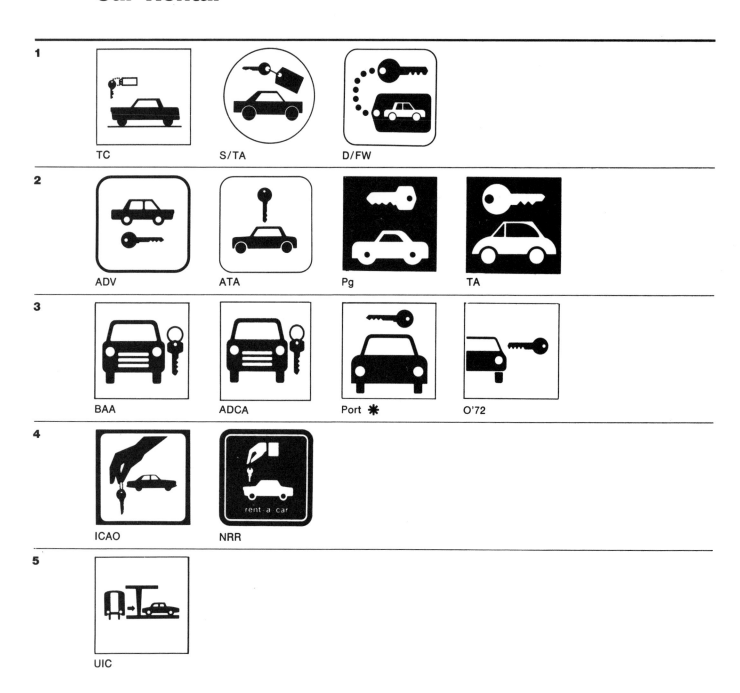

1
TC   S/TA   D/FW

2
ADV   ATA   Pg   TA

3
BAA   ADCA   Port ✳   O'72

4
ICAO   NRR

5
UIC

Concept Description	Symbol Source	Evaluation				Symbol Design Recommendations
		Semantic	Syntactic	Pragmatic	Group	
1 **Key with tag and side view of car.**	TC S/TA D/FW	3 3 3	2 3 3	2 3 3	4	We recommend that the Car Rental message be represented by a front view of an automobile with a large key above it, like the Port drawing in Group 3.
2 **Key and side view of car.**	ADV ATA Pg TA	3 3 4 4	3 3 3 3	3 3 4 3	4	
3 **Key and front view of car.**	BAA ADCA Port O'72	4 4 4 3	4 4 4 3	5 5 5 3	4	
4 **Hand holding key and side view of car.**	ICAO NRR	2 2	2 2	2 2	2	
5 **Train platform and arrow pointing toward car.**	UIC	1	2	1	1	

We believe that the key should not have a tag attached and that it should be horizontal, since a vertical key tends to resemble a standing figure. The key should be larger in relation to the car than it is in the Port drawing.

A standard representation of an automobile should be used for this message as well as for Taxi. These two drawings, however, should be detailed to maintain the distinction between these two messages. The drawing of the key in this symbol should be identical to the key used in the Baggage Locker drawing.

Summary:
Adopt Group 3 concept, with key above modified standard car drawing, as in Port version.

Restaurant

1

SP

IATA

UIC

BAA

ICAO

NRR

2

Port

ADV

Pg

TA

ADCA

D/FW

3

S/TA

TA ✳

WO'72

O'68

NPS

4

LVA

TC

X'67

O'72

KFAI

Concept Description	Symbol Source	Evaluation				Symbol Design Recommendations
		Semantic	Syntactic	Pragmatic	Group	
1 **Crossed utensils, spoon and fork or knife and fork.**	SP	4	4	4	**5**	It is impossible to use a symbol to describe the specific menus of various eating places. Therefore, we propose that only two symbols, reflecting opposite ends of the price scale, be used to represent food concessions. One to represent Restaurant and the other to represent Coffee Shop and Snack Bar.
	IATA	4	3	3		
	UIC	4	3	3		
	BAA	4	3	3		
	ICAO	4	2	3		
	NRR	4	3	3		

Although the crossed knife and fork are widely used throughout Europe to represent the general availability of food, the X shape is confusing because it has some connotation of prohibition.

In our judgment a drawing showing simply two or three utensils, like those in Group 2, is effective. It is a bold image that suggests a placesetting, and is sufficiently formal to avoid confusion with the Coffee Shop symbol.

Concept Description	Symbol Source	Evaluation				Symbol Design Recommendations
2 **Vertical knife and fork.**	Port	4	2	3	**4**	The utensils should be boldly drawn to be easily recognizable. We prefer those of the well proportioned TA symbol in Group 3. We think that two utensils are sufficient and that the fork should have four prongs.
	ADV	4	2	3		
	Pg	4	3	4		
	TA	4	2	3		
	ADCA	4	4	4		
	D/FW	5	4	4		

Summary:
Adopt Group 2 concept, with drawings of knife and fork similar to the TA symbol in Group 3.

Concept Description	Symbol Source	Evaluation				
3 **Vertical utensils, inside a circle.**	S/TA	4	3	3	**5**	
	O'64	4	3	4		
	TA	5	4	4		
	WO'72	5	4	4		
	O'68	4	3	4		
	NPS	5	3	4		

Concept Description	Symbol Source	Evaluation				
4 **Placesetting, utensils beside plate.**	LVA	4	2	2	**5**	
	TC	4	2	2		
	X'67	4	2	2		
	O'72	4	3	3		
	KFAI	4	4	3		

Coffee Shop

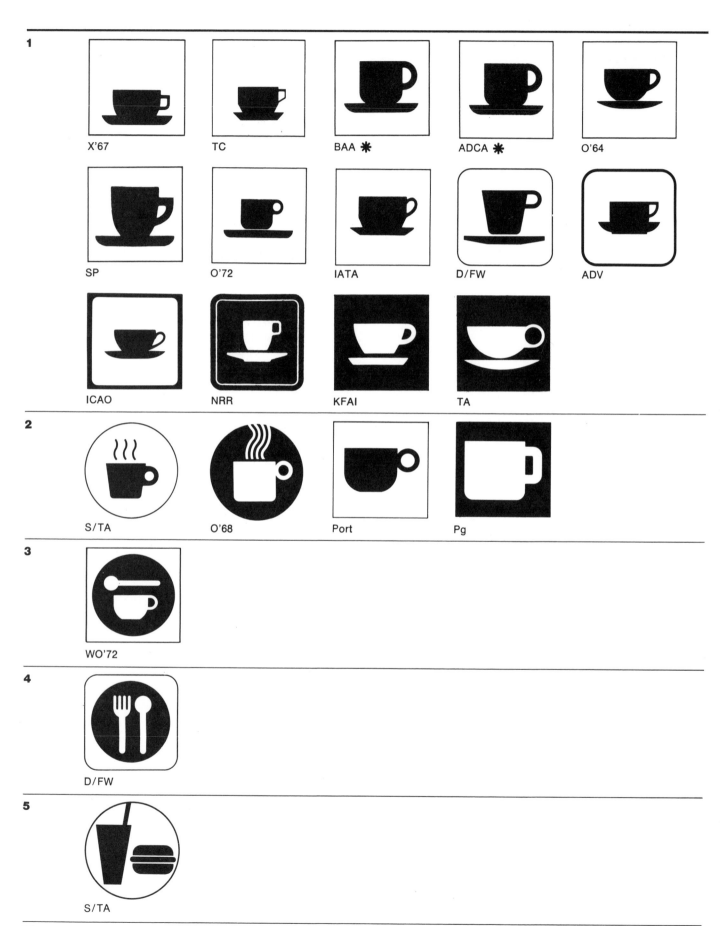

1

X'67

TC

BAA ✳

ADCA ✳

O'64

SP

O'72

IATA

D/FW

ADV

ICAO

NRR

KFAI

TA

2

S/TA

O'68

Port

Pg

3

WO'72

4

D/FW

5

S/TA

Concept Description	Symbol Source	Evaluation				Symbol Design Recommendations
		Semantic	Syntactic	Pragmatic	Group	
1 **Side view of cup and saucer.**	X'67	4	3	3	**5**	It is impossible to use a symbol to describe the specific menus of various eating places. Therefore, we propose that only two symbols, reflecting opposite ends of the price scale, be used to represent food concessions. One to represent Restaurant and the other to represent Coffee Shop and Snack Bar.
	TC	4	2	3		
	BAA	5	5	5		
	ADCA	5	4	5		
	O'64	4	3	3		
	SP	4	3	3		A side view of a coffee cup is a well established representation for Coffee Shop and it should be adopted to represent informal eating situations. Pictures of hamburgers, spoons, and milk shakes are unnecessary.
	O'72	5	2	4		
	IATA	5	3	4		
	D/FW	4	3	3		
	ADV	4	3	3		
	ICAO	4	3	3		The BAA drawing in Group 1 is very strong and clear. We suggest experimenting with a separation between the cup and saucer, as shown in the O'72 version.
	NRR	4	3	3		
	KFAI	4	4	3		
	TA	4	3	3		
2 **Side view of cup.**	S/TA	4	3	3	**5**	
	O'68	4	4	4		
	Port	4	4	4		
	Pg	4	3	3		
3 **Side view of cup with spoon.**	WO'72	4	3	3	**4**	
4 **Vertical utensils inside circle.**	D/FW	3	3	3	**3**	
5 **Burger and shake.**	S/TA	3	2	2	**3**	

Summary:
Adopt Group 1 concept, modify BAA symbol with separation between cup and saucer.

Bar

1

S/TA BAA ADCA Port

TC UIC D/FW Pg

2

ICAO

3

O'72

Concept Description	Symbol Source	Evaluation				Symbol Design Recommendations
		Semantic	Syntactic	Pragmatic	Group	
1 **Side view of a bar glass.**	S/TA	4	3	3	**5**	A side view of a bar glass is a well established symbol concept to represent Bar.
	BAA	4	5	4		
	ADCA	4	5	4		The committee believes that the glass should be shaped like a martini glass because other shapes have different uses and therefore invite confusion. The martini glass is strictly a bar glass.
	Port	4	4	3		
	TC	4	2	3		
	UIC	4	2	3		
	D/FW	5	4	4		We think that the glass should be boldly drawn like the BAA symbol but we are unsatisfied with its shape. Perhaps the Port version would be satisfactory if its stem and base were bolder.
	Pg	4	4	3		
						We suggest that the inclusion of a large dot representing an olive or cherry, like those in the D/FW or Port symbols, could help to reinforce the message.
2 **Side view of bar glasses.**	ICAO	4	2	2	**2**	**Summary:** **Adopt Group 1 concept, using bold version of martini glass with olive.**
3 **Side view of bar glass with fruit.**	O'72	3	2	2	**2**	

Shops

O'72

O'64

S/TA

Pg

TÅ

O'68

2

WO'72

D/FW

3

D/FW

4

S/TA

5

O'72

Pg

NRR

6

TC

Concept Description	Symbol Source	Evaluation				Symbol Design Recommendations
		Semantic	Syntactic	Pragmatic	Group	
1 **Perspective view of gift box.**	O'72	3	3	3	**3**	We believe that the effectiveness of the initial group of messages will be seriously diminished by attempts to encompass too many services and activities. In this regard we feel that it would be a mistake to try to create drawings for specific retail activities because they are not essential as processing activities or basic public services. In addition, retail activities are by their nature usually evident and located in prominent locations.
	O'64	3	4	4		
	S/TA	3	3	3		
	Pg	3	4	4		
	TA	3	3	3		
	O'68	3	4	3		
2 **Side view of gift box.**	WO'72	3	4	3	**3**	For cases where retail activities are completely out of sight, we suggest a symbol for the general category, Shops. The Shops symbol might contain elements from the Gift and Newsstand symbols collected in the inventory. We feel that the combination of gift box, pipe, and book or magazine would be a good starting point.
	D/FW	3	4	4		
3 **Newspaper, pipe, and cigarettes.**	D/FW	3	4	4	**3**	
4 **Newspapers.**	S/TA	2	1	2	**2**	
5 **Book.**	O'72	3	3	4	**3**	
	Pg	3	4	4		
	NRR	3	4	4		
6 **Books.**	TC	2	2	3	**2**	

Summary:
Develop new broad-purpose symbol combining gift box, pipe, and book or magazine.

Barber Shop

1

ADV

FA

O'72

TC

2

UIC

NRR

3

D/FW

Port

Pg

Concept Description	Symbol Source	Evaluation				Symbol Design Recommendations
		Semantic	Syntactic	Pragmatic	Group	
1 **Comb and open scissors**	ADV	4	3	4	**4**	The Committee agreed that the comb/scissors combination as shown in Group 1, is a well accepted symbol of Barber Shop and Beauty Salon. Like the Restaurant symbol with knife and fork, the implements should be shown side by side, as in FA, rather than overlapping, as in UIC. Since the opened scissors form implies an X with possible "No" connotations, the closed form (as in Port and Pg) is preferable.
	FA	4	4	4		
	O'72	4	4	4		
	TC	4	3	3		
2 **Open scissors crossed over a comb**	UIC	4	3	3	**3**	We feel that the same symbol can be used for both Barber Shop and Beauty Salon with the appropriate standard figure added (as in Group 3 concept) only where needed to distinguish between the two.
	NRR	3	3	3		
3 **Comb, scissors and standing man**	D/FW	4	2	4	**4**	**Summary:** **Adopt Group 1 concept, but with closed scissor. Add standard male figure where needed to distinguish from Beauty Salon.**
	Port	4	3	3		
	Pg	4	3	4		

Beauty Salon

D/FW

Pg

Port

Concept Description	Symbol Source	Evaluation				Symbol Design Recommendations
		Semantic	Syntactic	Pragmatic	Group	
1 **Comb, scissors and standing woman**	D/FW	3	3	4	**3**	See recommendation for Barber Shop.
	Pg	3	3	3		
	Port	3	3	3		

Summary:
Use same scissors/comb symbol described in recommendation for Barber Shop. Add standard female figure where needed to distinguish from Barber Shop.

Ticket Purchase

1

ICAO

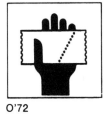
D/FW

ATA

2

O'64

WO'72

O'72

3

UIC

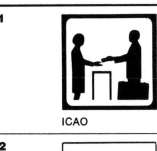
NRR

4

LVA

Concept Description	Symbol Source	Evaluation				Symbol Design Recommendations
		Semantic	Syntactic	Pragmatic	Group	
1 **Figures exchanging ticket over a counter.**	ICAO	2	2	2	**2**	The committee believes that the ideal symbol for this message would be a ticket. Unfortunately actual tickets used for various transportation modes vary greatly in size, shape, and complexity. Because of this, it is difficult to create a drawing of a ticket that is appropriate to all modes. The drawings of tickets in Groups 2 and 3 fail as all-purpose indicators.
	D/FW	2	2	2		
	ATA	2	2	2		
2 **Hand holding a ticket.**	O'64	2	3	3	**2**	In fact, none of the existing symbols are entirely adequate representations of the complex message, Ticket Purchase. Therefore, we recommend experimenting with two different approaches.
	WO'72	2	3	3		
	O'72	2	3	2		1 Begin with the concept represented in Group 1 and create a simplified drawing of it.
3 **Tickets.**	UIC	3	3	3	**3**	2 Take the concept represented in Group 4, hands exchanging money and ticket, and attempt to simplify it and produce a drawing that is compatible with the others in the initial group.
	NRR	2	2	2		
4 **Hands exchanging money and tickets.**	LVA	4	4	4	**4**	**Summary:** **Experiment with clarifying and simplifying both Group 1 and Group 4 concepts.**

Baggage Check-in

1

BAA

ADCA

Port

ICAO

UIC

O'72

NRR

TC

2

S/TA

ATA

3

D/FW

Concept Description	Symbol Source	Evaluation				Symbol Design Recommendations
		Semantic	Syntactic	Pragmatic	Group	
1 **Suitcase sitting on scale.**	BAA	5	5	5	**5**	Ordinarily Baggage Check-in is considered along with Baggage Claim as a related pair of symbols, even though they are usually at opposite ends of the travel experience.
	ADCA	5	5	5		
	Port	5	4	4		
	ICAO	5	2	3		
	UIC	5	4	4		We believe that a bold drawing of a suitcase sitting on a weighing scale is a good representation of Baggage Check-in at airports. The BAA and ADCA drawings are strong examples. Unfortunately the scale is inappropriate for all but international travel. It is obviously the wrong image for certain procedures such as curb-side check-in.
	O'72	5	3	4		
	NRR	4	3	3		
	TC	4	2	3		

In view of this, and because of the infrequent need to represent this activity, we believe that a picture of a suitcase alone can be used to communicate both Baggage Check-in and Baggage Claim.

Concept Description	Symbol Source	Evaluation				Symbol Design Recommendations
2 **Figure, suitcase, and arrow pointing away.**	S/TA	2	3	3	**2**	A standard representation of a suitcase should be established and consistently used for these messages as well as for Baggage Locker. See Baggage Locker recommendations for advice on how to draw a suitcase.
	ATA	2	3	3		

Summary:
Use standard drawing of suitcase.

Concept Description	Symbol Source	Evaluation				
3 **Arrow pointing from suitcase toward plane.**	D/FW	3	3	2	**2**	

Baggage Claim

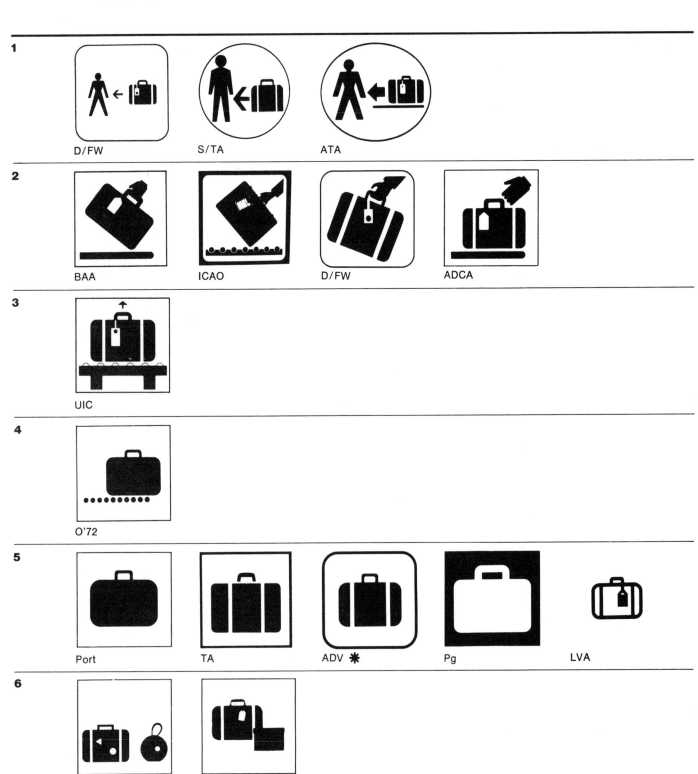

1

D/FW   S/TA   ATA

2

BAA   ICAO   D/FW   ADCA

3

UIC

4

O'72

5

Port   TA   ADV ✳   Pg   LVA

6

TC   IATA

Concept Description	Symbol Source	Evaluation				Symbol Design Recommendations
		Semantic	Syntactic	Pragmatic	Group	
1 **Arrow pointing from suitcase toward man.**	D/FW S/TA ATA	3 3 3	3 3 3	3 3 3	**3**	We believe that this message is most directly and effectively conveyed by a picture of a suitcase, such as the symbols in the fifth group. The ADV drawing is a good example of this concept.
						Conveyor belts and hands are complicated and unnecessary. Neither of the visual devices contributes appreciably to the meaning. Is the hand lifting the suitcase or putting it down?
2 **Hand holding suitcase.**	BAA ICAO D/FW ADCA	5 4 5 5	4 3 4 4	4 3 4 4	**4**	The drawing of the suitcase should be the same as the one developed for the messages Baggage Check-in and Baggage Lockers.
						Summary: **Adopt Group 5 concept, modifying ADV version to reflect standard suitcase drawing.**
3 **Suitcase on conveyor, arrow pointing up.**	UIC	4	3	3	**4**	
4 **Suitcase on conveyor.**	O'72	4	4	4	**4**	
5 **Suitcase.**	Port TA ADV Pg LVA	4 4 4 4 3	4 4 4 4 3	4 4 4 4 3	**4**	
6 **Suitcases.**	TC IATA	3 3	2 2	3 3	**3**	

Customs

1

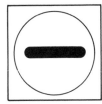

BAA

2

UIC ADV

3

D/FW

4

Pg

5

O'72 ✳ TC

Concept Description	Symbol Source	Evaluation				Symbol Design Recommendations
		Semantic	Syntactic	Pragmatic	Group	
1 **Customs symbol.**	BAA	2	4	4	**1**	This message is closely related to Immigration and the symbols developed should reinforce this relationship. The committee recommends using the concept shown in Group 5, an inspector examining an open suitcase. Redrawing to relate this symbol to the others in the initial group will be needed.
2 **Suitcase with customs symbol.**	UIC ADV	2 3	3 3	3 3	**3**	This symbol could be used adjacent to the Immigration drawing to represent Inspection Services. **Summary:** **Adopt Group 5 concept, with simplified drawing of inspector and open suitcase.**
3 **Suitcase with US Government Seal.**	D/FW	4	4	4	**4**	
4 **Suitcase and big eye.**	Pg	3	4	4	**1**	
5 **Inspector examining suitcase.**	O'72 TC	3 4	4 3	4 3	**4**	

Immigration

1

Pg

2

D/FW

3

S/TA   ATA

4

O'72 ✱   TC

Concept Description	Symbol Source	Evaluation				Symbol Design Recommendations
		Semantic	Syntactic	Pragmatic	Group	
1 **Rubber stamp.**	Pg	2	4	3	**2**	This message is closely related to Customs and the symbols developed should reinforce this relationship. The committee recommends the concept represented by the drawings in Group 4, an inspector examining an open passport. This symbol could be used adjacent to the Customs drawing to represent Inspection Services. **Summary:** **Adopt Group 4 concept, with simplified drawing of inspector and passport.**
2 **Hand holding rubber stamp and US Government Seal above.**	D/FW	4	3	4	**4**	
3 **US Government Seal.**	S/TA ATA	4 4	3 3	4 4	**2**	
4 **Inspector examining passport.**	O'72 TC	4 3	4 3	4 4	**4**	

Departing Flights

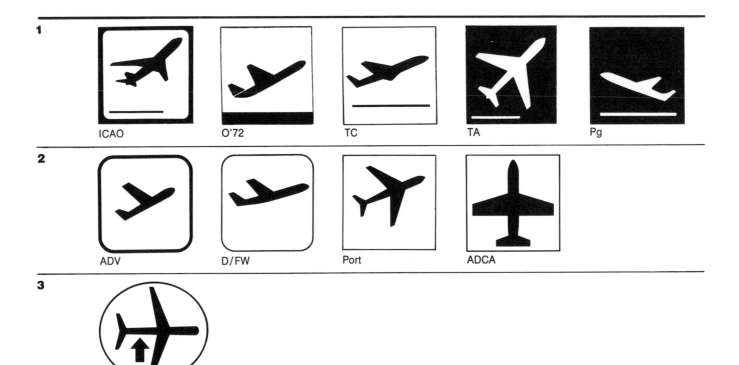

1 ICAO | O'72 | TC | TA | Pg

2 ADV | D/FW | Port | ADCA

3

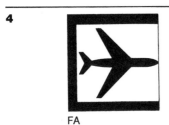

ATA

4 FA

Concept Description	Symbol Source	Evaluation				Symbol Design Recommendations
		Semantic	Syntactic	Pragmatic	Group	
1 **Ascending airplane with ground line**	ICAO	4	3	4	**4**	This message, which is used almost exclusively on approach roads and ramps, is best portrayed by a silhouette of a plane pointing diagonally up. We prefer the boldness of the TA symbol, but feel that the bottom "ground line" is not necessary, and inappropriate for this kind of full silhouette.
	O'72	4	3	3		
	TC	4	3	4		
	TA	3	3	3		
	Pg	4	4	4		
2 **Ascending airplane**	ADV	3	3	3	**4**	The standard airplane drawing used for Air Transportation should be utilized here.
	D/FW	3	3	3		
	Port	2	2	3		**Summary:** **Adopt TA design, eliminating ground line.**
	ADCA	2	3	3		
3 **Horizontal airplane and arrow pointing up**	ATA	2	2	2	**2**	
4 **Horizontal airplane within box, facing out**	FA	1	3	2	**1**	

Arriving Flights

1

ADV

ICAO

O'72

Pg

TA

TC

2

D/FW

Port

3

ATA

4

FA

Concept Description	Symbol Source	Evaluation				Symbol Design Recommendations
		Semantic	Syntactic	Pragmatic	Group	
1 **Descending airplane with ground line**	ADV	3	3	3	**3**	This message causes considerable confusion. It is almost always used in conjunction with the message "Departing Flights" on approach roads and ramps. The confusion is partly verbal; you are "arriving" at the airport in another mode of transportation, but might want to "depart" in a plane, or meet someone else who is "arriving". While airport personnel understand the distinction, there seems to be agreement that the public, especially those who do not use airports regularly, have to pause to determine whether they want the "arrivals" or "departures" ramp. And it presents a danger because this point of confusion usually occurs at a critical roadway intersection.
	ICAO	3	2	3		
	O'72	3	3	3		
	Pg	3	3	3		
	TA	2	3	2		
	TC	3	3	3		
						There is also a visual problem, because the concept of an airplane pointed at the ground, as shown in Groups 1 and 2, threateningly implies "crashing" to some people, and causes anxiety. (And, of course, in reality a plane actually lands in the opposite attitude from that shown.)
2 **Descending airplane**	D/FW	3	3	2	**2**	
	Port	2	2	2		For these reasons, and because the real reason one takes the "arrivals" ramp is to meet an incoming passenger (not plane), we recommend that the concept be changed to "Passenger Pick-Up" and that a symbol be developed which portrays a passenger whose arm is raised in greeting or hailing an unseen person or taxi.
3 **Horizontal airplane with arrow pointing down**	ATA	2	2	2	**2**	We believe that, used in conjunction with the rising airplane for Departing Flights, this new Passenger Pick-Up concept will help relieve some of the current confusion.
4 **Horizontal airplane within box, facing inside**	FA	2	2	2	**2**	**Summary:** **Develop new symbol, showing passenger with up-raised arm.**

Smoking

1

X'70

2

KFAI   Pg   UIC

3

O'68

Concept Description	Symbol Source	Evaluation				Symbol Design Recommendations
		Semantic	Syntactic	Pragmatic	Group	
1 **Hand holding burning cigarette.**	X'70	4	3	3	**4**	**Summary:** **The image for the Smoking symbol should be identical to that developed for No Smoking but without the prohibition symbol superimposed on it.**
2 **Burning cigarette.**	KFAI Pg UIC	5 5 5	3 3 3	4 4 3	**4**	
3 **Burning pipe.**	O'68	4	3	3	**3**	

No Smoking

1

O'72

X'70

2

Port

KFAI

ICAO

ADCA

TC

Pg

BAA

D/FW

TA

S/TA

3

UIC

ADV

4

O'68

5

X'67

NPS

6

ATA

IATA

Concept Description	Symbol Source	Evaluation				Symbol Design Recommendations
		Semantic	Syntactic	Pragmatic	Group	
1 **Hand holding burning cigarette, crossed out.**	O'72 X'70	4 4	3 3	3 3	**4**	In conformity with recently established official highway signs, the committee recommends the consistent use of the internationally accepted convention of a red circle with a red diagonal bar through it to represent prohibitions (except No Entry, which has a separate symbol).
2 **Burning cigarette, crossed out.**	Port KFAI ICAO ADCA TC Pg BAA D/FW TA S/TA	5 5 5 5 5 5 5 5 5 5	3 4 3 4 3 3 4 3 3 3	4 4 3 4 3 4 4 4 4 4	**5**	We propose the concept shown in Group 2, a red circle and red diagonal bar, from upper left to lower right, superimposed over a cigarette, We prefer a white cigarette but recognize that it may be impossible to draw boldly. Therefore, we will accept a solid line indication if it reads clearly.
3 **Burning cigarette, crossed out by X.**	UIC ADV	5 5	3 2	4 4	**5**	We are unsatisfied with the indications of smoke used in the symbols collected. We encourage experimentation with drawing less flame-like smoke with more definition of softly billowing forms. **Summary:** **Adopt Group 2 concept, with red circle and diagonal bar crossing out cigarette.**
4 **Burning pipe, crossed out.**	O'68	4	3	3	**4**	
5 **Burning match, crossed out.**	X'67 NPS	4	3	2	**4**	
6 **Cigarette, cigar, and pipe, crossed out.**	ATA IATA	4 4	3 3	3 3	**2**	

Parking

1

WO'72    S/TA

2

O'72    ATA    D/FW    KFAI  ✱   Pg

TA    NPS

3

NRR

4

TC

110

Concept Description	Symbol Source	Evaluation				Symbol Design Recommendations
		Semantic	Syntactic	Pragmatic	Group	
1 **Letter P and car.**	WO'72	3	2	2	**3**	The large letter P is becoming a standard symbol for this message. We recommend adoption of the Group 2 concept, the letter P inside a square. Other elements are unneccessary.
	S/TA	3	2	2		
2 **Letter P.**	O'72	3	4	4	**3**	The specific drawing of the letter should relate to the other drawings in the initial group of messages. The style and proportions of the KFAI drawing could serve as a starting point.
	ATA	3	4	4		
	D/FW	3	4	4		**Summary:**
	KFAI	3	4	4		**Adopt Group 2 concept of large letter P.**
	Pg	3	4	4		
	TA	3	4	4		
	NPS	3	4	4		
3 **Letter P combined with NRR logo.**	NRR	3	3	3		
4 **Letter P inside circle.**	TC	3	4	4	**3**	

No Parking

1

NPS

D/FW

O'72

2

Pg

Concept Description	Symbol Source	Evaluation				Symbol Design Recommendations
		Semantic	Syntactic	Pragmatic	Group	
1 **Letter P crossed out.**	NPS	3	4	4	**3**	As with No Smoking, we recommend adoption of the the international convention of indicating prohibition by superimposing a red circle with a red diagonal bar over the standard drawing.
	D/FW	3	4	4		
	O'72	3	4	4		The No Parking symbol should use the standard P created for the message Parking, reduced if necessary.
2 **Letter P combined with prohibition symbol.**	Pg	3	4	4	**4**	**Summary:** **Adopt concept represented by the Pg drawing in Group 2, the letter P combined with standard prohibition indicator.**

No Dogs

1

BAA   O'76   TC

2

CSS   KFAI

3

O'72

4

ADV

Concept Description	Symbol Source	Evaluation				Symbol Design Recommendations
		Semantic	Syntactic	Pragmatic	Group	
1 **Dog, crossed out by red diagonal line and circle**	BAA O'76 TC	3 4 4	3 3 3	3 3 4	**4**	We recommend adoption of the Group 1 concept, using the profile of a dog within a red circle with the standard diagonal prohibiting slash.

The Committee recommends that the dog face right, and be of an anonymous breed.

Summary: **Adopt Group 1 concept.** |
2 **Dog, crossed out by diagonal line**	CSS KFAI	3 4	3 3	3 4	**3**	
3 **Dog, crossed out by horizontal bar**	O'72	3	2	2	**3**	
4 **Dog, crossed out by X**	ADV	3	2	2	**3**	

Entrance

1

FA

2

O'72

O'76

3

UIC

X'67

KFAI

NRR

4

Pg

Concept Description	Symbol Source	Evaluation				Symbol Design Recommendations
		Semantic	Syntactic	Pragmatic	Group	
1 **Figure walking within open 3-sided box**	FA	1	3	2	**1**	Usually, the way to enter or proceed through a space is implied if there is no indication of prohibition, such as a No Entry sign. In other cases, the way can usually be correctly delineated by combining an arrow with the appropriate indication of what you will find at the destination.
2 **Figure proceeding towards vertical bar**	O'72 O'76	1 1	3 3	2 2	**1**	
3 **Arrow penetrating opening of box, pointing within**	UIC X'67 KFAI NRR	2 1 2 2	3 3 3 2	2 2 2 2	**2**	
4 **Arrow, outside, pointing to opening**	Pg	2	3	2	**2**	

Many existing systems use a special symbol for the message Entrance but the Committee feels that all of the existing symbols for this message are unsatisfactory. The Group 1 and 2 symbols are ambiguous, and almost identical to the "Exit" symbols from the same systems. The Group 3 symbols imply, to those who can understand diagrams, entry into an enclosed space. But this is often not the meaning intended. In addition, the arrow implies a direction to the side, whereas in fact, you will usually be proceeding ahead. Combining an arrow-dominated symbol sign, such as X'67, with a directional arrow pointing differently causes further confusion. The Group 4 symbol eliminates the enclosed box problem, but not the other concerns mentioned above.

In view of the fact that it is not often necessary to symbolize the message Entrance, and since no satisfactory symbols for it are currently in use, we recommend that no special symbol be adopted for this message.

Summary:
No special symbol needed for this message.

No Entry

TA

Pg

Port

IATA

BAA

D/FW

2

KFAI

S/TA

TC

ICAO

4

WO'72

X'70

5

UIC

NRR

6

ADV

Concept Description	Symbol Source	Evaluation				Symbol Design Recommendations
		Semantic	Syntactic	Pragmatic	Group	
1 **No Entry symbol.**	TA	5	5	5	**5**	In our judgment the internationally accepted road sign showing a white horizontal bar inside a red disk should be accepted for this message. The symbols in Group 1 are examples of this concept. They are very bold. We believe that the Port version is especially well proportioned in relation to its format.
	Pg	5	5	5		
	Port	5	5	5		
	IATA	5	4	5		
	BAA	5	4	5		
	D/FW	5	4	5		
2 **Upraised hand.**	X'67	3	4	4	**3**	
	KFAI	3	4	4		
3 **Standing figure, crossed out.**	S/TA	3	3	4	**2**	
	TC	3	2	4		
	ICAO	3	2	3		
4 **Standing figure, crossed out by X.**	WO'72	3	3	4	**2**	
	X'70	3	3	4		
5 **Standing figure with arms extended, inside a circle.**	UIC	2	2	3	**1**	
	NRR	2	2	3		
6 **Standing figure with arms extended, superimposed over No Entry symbol.**	ADV	1	2	2	**1**	

Summary:
Adopt Group 1 concept, maintain proper relation between bar and circle.

Exit

1

FA

2

O'72

O'76

3

UIC

KFAI

NRR

4

O'64

X'67

Pg

5

BAA

Concept Description	Symbol Source	Evaluation				Symbol Design Recommendations
		Semantic	Syntactic	Pragmatic	Group	
1 **Figure walking out of open 3-sided box**	FA	2	3	2	**1**	The word Exit, because of its mandated use in public buildings throughout the U.S., is well recognized by Americans to mean "the way out". This fact would seem to suggest the advisability of simply using the word EXIT as the symbol.
2 **Figure proceeding away from vertical bar**	O'72	2	3	2	**1**	Yet, unlike words such as HOTEL or TAXI, the word EXIT is little used outside of English-speaking countries. Sortie, Ausgang, Salida—all have the same meaning in other widely-used languages.
	O'76	2	3	2		The idea of Exit is a fairly abstract concept, difficult to show as an image, as can be seen from the examples shown. The Group 1 and 2 symbols are ambiguous. Groups 3 and 4 imply, to those who can read diagrams, exit from an enclosed space. But this is sometimes not the meaning intended. More importantly, the arrow implies a direction to the side, whereas in fact one usually must proceed ahead. Combining an arrow dominated symbol such as X'67 with a directional arrow pointing differently would cause considerable confusion.
3 **Arrows penetrating opening of box and pointing out**	UIC	2	3	2	**2**	
	KFAI	2	2	2		
	NRR	2	2	2		
4 **Arrows within boxes, pointing to opening**	O'64	2	2	2	**2**	The group 5 symbol, used at London (Heathrow) Airport, seems to us a much better direction, especially since it is complimentary to the standard No Entry symbol from the primary group. Whereas the No Entry symbol is a red ("Stop") disk with a horizontal bar (a barrier), the Exit symbol is a green ("go") disk with a vertical bar (raised barrier). To further imply the idea of passageway, the vertical bar completely bisects the green disk.
	X'67	2	2	2		
	Pg	2	3	2		
5 **Green disk, vertically bisected**	BAA	3	4	5	**4**	As with the No Entry symbol, this is abstract in concept, and would require a good deal of exposure before being understood. To overcome this problem, we recommend that, for a number of years, the symbol be combined with the appropriate word (in the U.S., with EXIT) to designate an exit. Common use of a single symbolic device with the appropriate local wording would make the message clear to both the resident and the international traveler. Additionally, after an extended period of time, the symbol would have sufficient exposure to stand on its own, without the use of any words.

Summary:
Adopt Group 5 concept of a vertically bisected green disk.

Fire Extinguisher

1

D/FW

2

Pg

Concept Description	Symbol Source	Evaluation				Symbol Design Recommendations
		Semantic	Syntactic	Pragmatic	Group	
1 **Fire extinguisher with flared nozzle**	D/FW	4	3	4	**4**	The profile of a fire extinguisher seems an obvious concept for this message. We feel that the D/FW symbol has more the sense of an industrial extinguisher than does the Pg symbol, but could be simplified and made more active in appearance. **Summary:** **Adopt Group 1 concept.**
2 **Fire extinguisher with hose and nozzle in resting position**	Pg	4	2	4	**3**	

Litter Disposal

1

O'68

SP

2

UIC

3

O'72

4

Mr. Pitch-In

Concept Description	Symbol Source	Evaluation				Symbol Design Recommendations
		Semantic	Syntactic	Pragmatic	Group	
1 **Trash entering receptacle**	O'68 SP	2 2	2 2	2 2	**2**	This sign will be affixed to the receptacle, rather than showing the way to it. In this sense it is different from all other symbols in the system.
2 **Hand, trash and receptacle**	UIC	2	2	2	**2**	
3 **Arrow pointing down into ellipse**	O'72	2	2	2	**2**	
4 **Mr. Pitch-In**						

We do not find any of the concepts shown to be totally effective, and recommend experimentation with two approaches:

1. Show a figure in the act of disposing a container as in the Pitch-In symbol, but in a less cartoon-like drawing.

2. Show a more symbolic upright container shape, with a strong curved arrow pointing down into it.

Summary:
Develop new symbol with figure disposing trash in container, or upright container with down-pointing arrow.

3

Recommended Symbols

In attempting to establish a unified set of symbols, one of the goals was to draw the symbols so they had a single graphic vocabulary. This was especially difficult in this project because of the extreme variety of images required by the messages. Some of the messages can be represented by bold abstract forms which depend on widespread education to become conventional symbols, such as the red cross or the internationally accepted No Entry symbol. Others depend on a picture of an object that is closely associated with the message to carry the meaning, such as airplane for Air Transportation or coffee cup for Coffee Shop. Finally, there are messages that are actually complex pictures of people engaged in processes such as purchasing a ticket, riding in an elevator, or inspecting luggage. Nevertheless, all the symbols, simple and complex, must function as a group with a recognizable visual vocabulary.

Fortunately there are basic visual devices that can help establish a unified graphic vocabulary among the symbols. Many of these devices were employed in the creation of the initial group of symbols.

Simplification of the images is one characteristic that makes the set of symbols a coherent group. The amount of detail used in the drawings has been reduced to a practical minimum. Unimportant features have been eliminated, resulting in a set of symbols that are consistently bold and direct. This characteristic boldness is also important if the symbols are to function as signs in busy confusing environments where unnecessary details would reduce legibility.

Because the symbols are frequently constructed with lines, the drawings use an optically consistent line weight to create unity. Line elements, like the envelope, umbrella handle and elevator are examples of the use of this device.

The edges of many of the forms have been softened with curves to create contours that are distinctive and help to establish visual relationships throughout the group of drawings. Examples of this technique are the rounded edges on the base of the bar glass, the edges of the elevator, the tires on the bus and cars, and the legs and arms of the figures.

The symbols were all drawn to function as dark figures on a light background. Wherever possible the forms were made as symmetrical shapes with a vertical center axis. In addition, each symbol was drawn to be placed within a unified format, a square with rounded corners.

The individual drawings for each symbol and the entire set of symbols were constantly reviewed and compared by Cook and Shanosky and the AIGA committee during the intensive period of development. The Department of Transportation's Advisory Committee also contributed evaluations during this time. Alternative versions were frequently considered and numerous detailed revisions were pursued as the set of final drawings evolved.

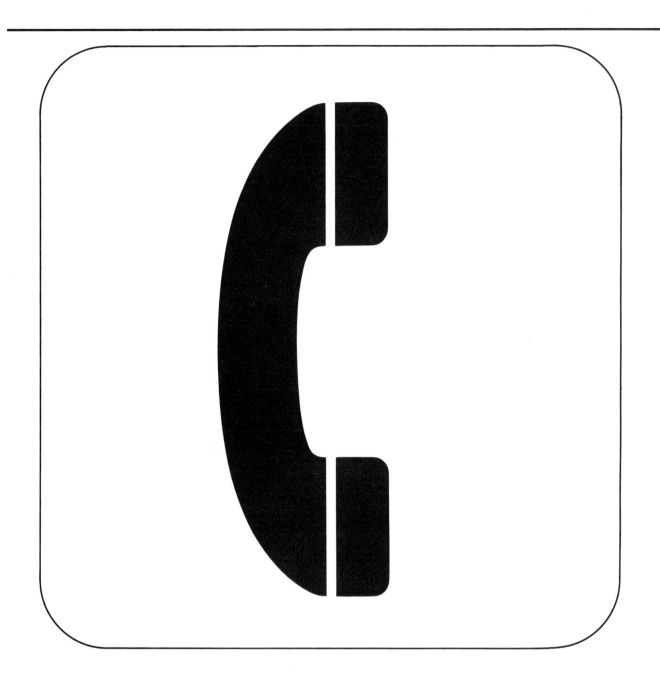

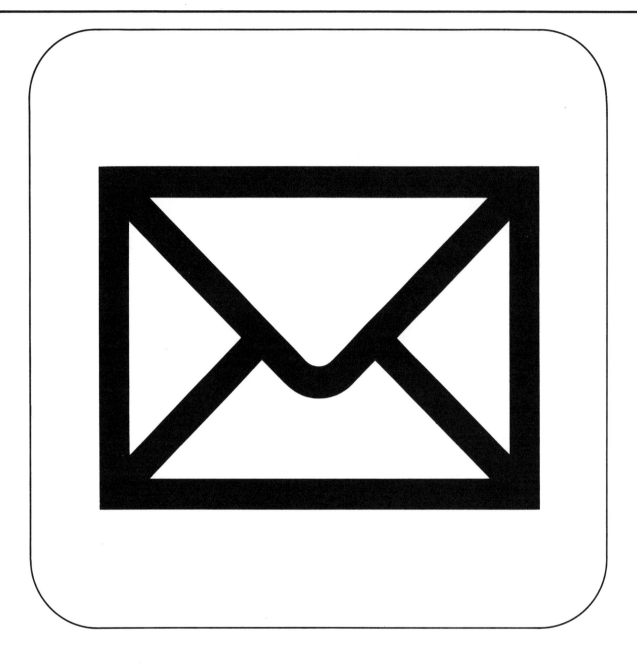

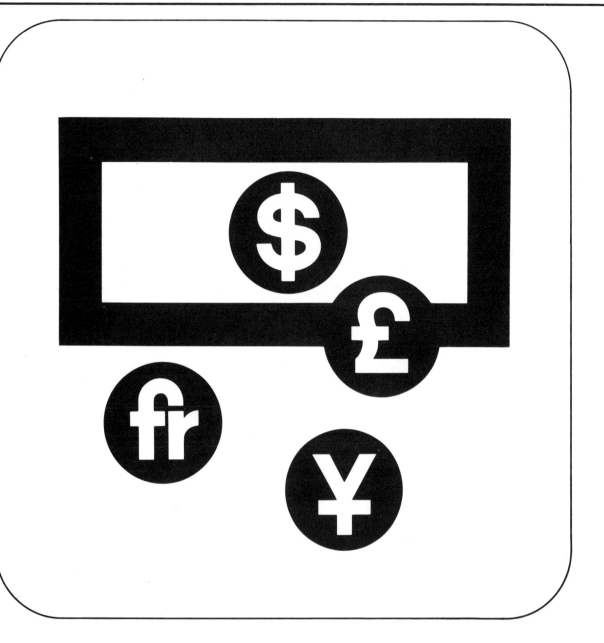

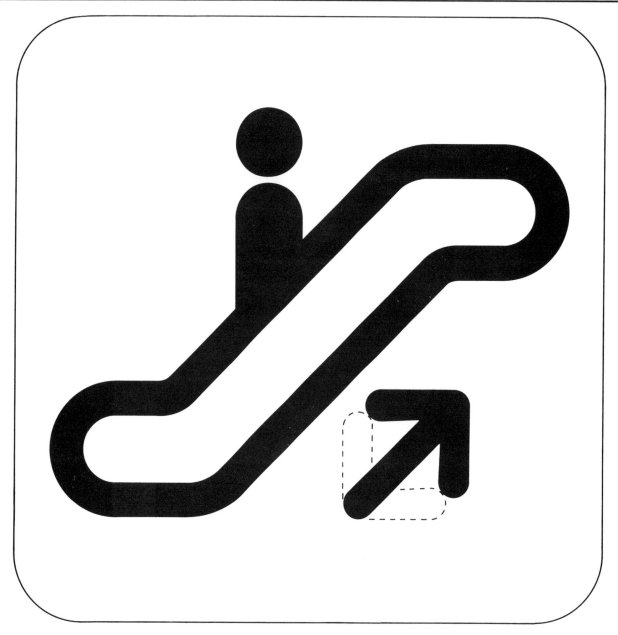

It is recommended that signing systems use the general Escalator symbol shown on the previous page wherever possible and resort to the "Up" and "Down" versions only if absolutely necessary, because these versions when combined with separate directional arrows can be confusing.

Usually the general Escalator symbol and a separate directional arrow can point the way to an escalator system which is not visible or a great distance away. On arrival at the system, pedestrians can usually be guided by directional arrows only, since the escalators themselves are usually visible.

The "Up" and "Down" combination versions shown on this page should be used only when the general Escalator symbol plus separate directional arrows are not sufficient, such as when it is necessary to clearly point the direction to the Up escalator alone, and the escalator itself is not visible.

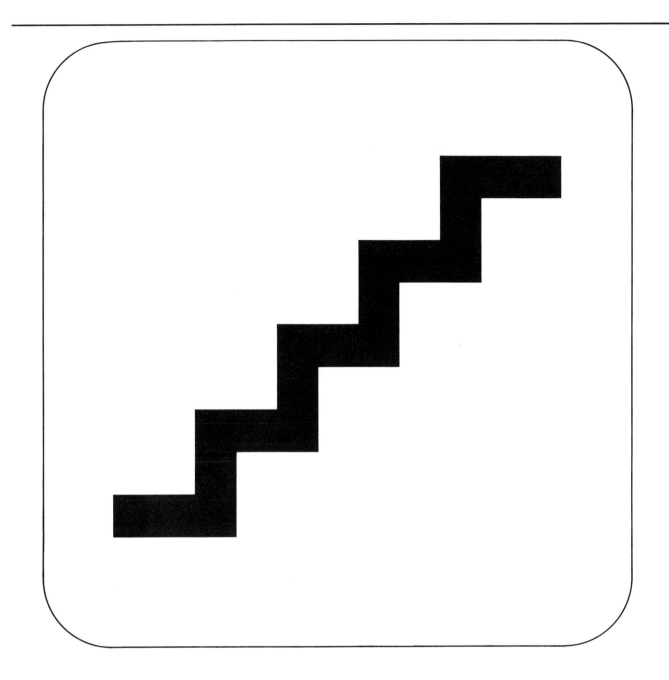

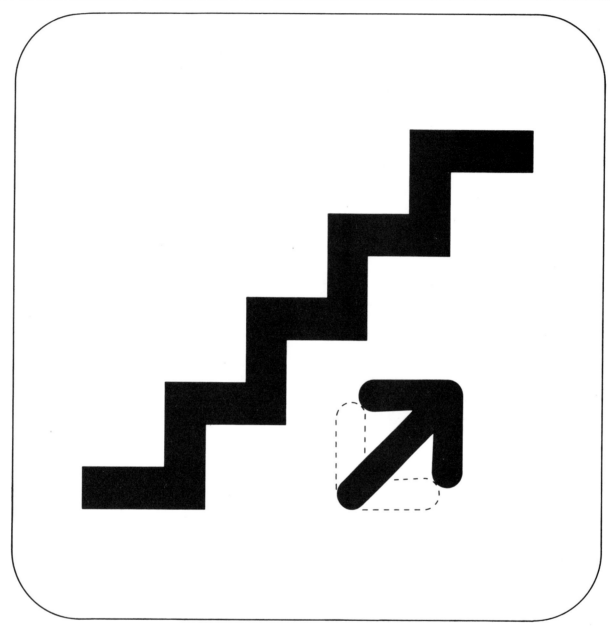

It is usually not necessary to indicate stair direction, since by their very nature stairs can be negotiated up and down. The combination symbols shown on this page should be used only when there is a strong reason to indicate the direction of movement on the stairs.

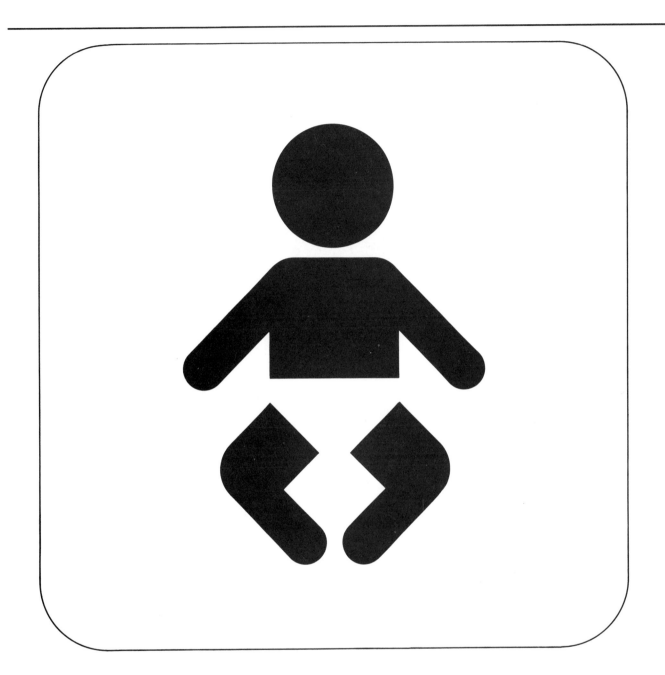

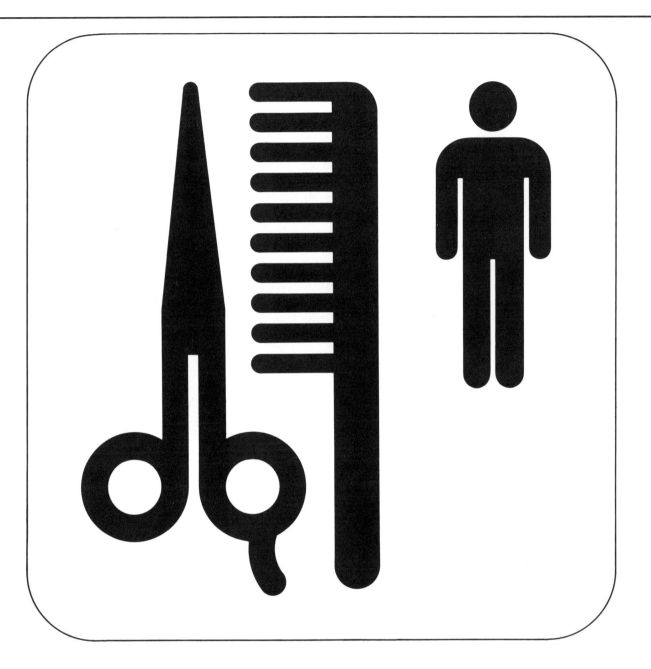

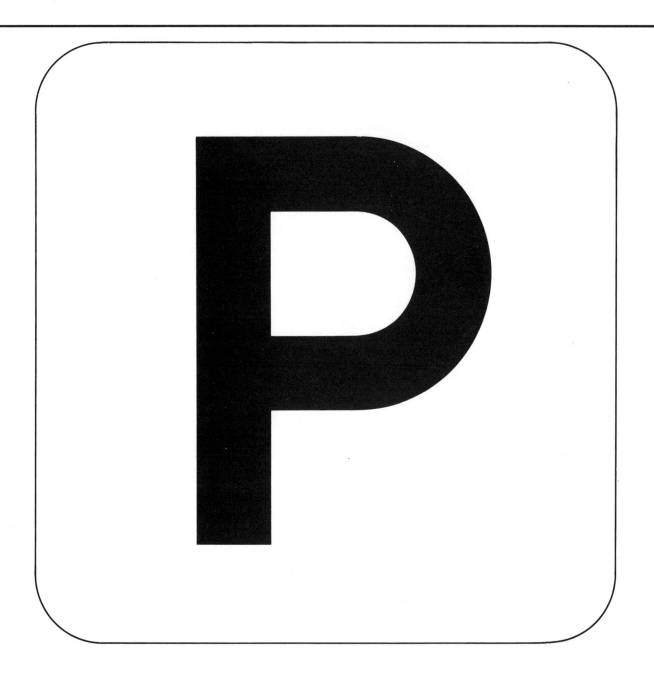

To indicate areas of access for handicapped
people, we recommend use of the official
International Symbol of Access for the
Handicapped, placed within the standard square
sign field recommended in this report.
Information about the symbol is available from:
The President's Committee on Employment of
the Handicapped,
Washington, D.C. 20210

Symbol Signs System

Public Services

1	Telephone
2	Mail
3	Currency Exchange
4	Cashier
5	First Aid
6	Lost and Found
7	Coat Check
8	Baggage Lockers
9	Escalator
10	Stairs
11	Elevator
12	Toilets, Men
13	Toilets, Women
14	Toilets
15	Nursery
16	Drinking Fountain
17	Waiting Room
18	Information
19	Hotel Information
20	Air Transportation
21	Heliport
22	Taxi
23	Bus
24	Ground Transportation
25	Rail Transportation
26	Water Transportation

Concessions

27	Car Rental
28	Restaurant
29	Coffee Shop
30	Bar
31	Shops
32	Barber Shop/Beauty Salon
33	Barber Shop
34	Beauty Salon

Processing Activities

35	Ticket Purchase
36	Baggage Check-in
37	Baggage Claim
38	Customs
39	Immigration
40	Departing Flights
41	Arriving Flights

Regulations

42	Smoking
43	No Smoking
44	Parking
45	No Parking
46	No Dogs
47	No Entry
48	Exit
49	Fire Extinguisher
50	Litter Disposal

4

Guidelines

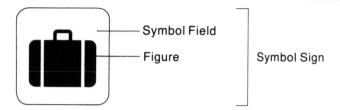

Symbol Field

Figure

Symbol Sign

The following guidelines were developed to illustrate desirable applications of the symbols to signage. The intent is not to provide a rigid set of rules, but rather a suggested range of possibilities within which the problems most commonly encountered in facility signage can be resolved without sacrificing the integrity of the symbol system.

From the standpoint of legibility and recognition, 'ideal' guidelines would advocate universal consistency in presentation (including layout, accompanying letter style, arrow, size relationship, color relationship, illumination and conformity to an established size/distance formula).

However, cultural, environmental and architectural conditions and styles vary greatly. Thus, from an aesthetic point of view, an 'ideal' set of guidelines would advocate freedom of application to allow and encourage the integration of graphics into the visual fabric of the environment.

These two ideals appear to be in conflict, but in fact need not be. Experienced designers know that the same visual elements may function entirely differently in different surroundings. For example, a yellow panel will stand out powerfully on a dark grey wall, be less forceful on a white wall, and disappear entirely on a yellow wall; or, a modern sans-serif letter style that may be in harmony with the contemporary architecture of a modern airport, may be dissonant in an environment like Colonial Williamsburg.

With these thoughts in mind, the guidelines that follow were developed to achieve the following goals:

To ensure legibility.

To aid in the process of learning to 'read' the symbols.

To provide adequate flexibility to allow appropriate response to specific design problems.

Well conceived and handsomely designed symbol signs will not be effective as communication unless they are thoughtfully and carefully applied.

But determining *how* to use the symbol signs is more easily prescribed than deciding *when* to use them. The following opinions, quoted from the initial reports, are still valid:

The effectiveness of symbols is strictly limited. They are most effective when they represent a service or concession that can be represented by an object, such as a bus or bar glass. They are much less effective when used to represent a process or activity, such as Ticket Purchase, because these are complex interactions that vary considerably from mode to mode and even from carrier to carrier.

Symbols are useless at a facility unless incorporated as part of an intelligent total sign system. The use of symbols alone, without consideration for the verbal messages and all other signing, will only add to the confusion.

It is more harmful to oversign than to undersign. To mix messages about relatively insignificant activities and concessions with essential public messages weakens the communication. The use of too many symbols at one time is counterproductive.

Legibility Criteria

The following diagram illustrates the results of pragmatic testing of several symbols (Ticket Purchase, Elevator, and Taxi) and represents a rough guide to size/distance relationships.

For the purpose of this illustration 'legibility' was defined as the recognition of the various elements that make the symbol understandable without the aid of wording or preconditioning. ('Recognition' of the symbols after they are learned is another matter which cannot be meaningfully tested at this time except in the case of those few well known symbols such as First Aid, Men, Women, etc.) The testing was done in daylight using symbols with black figures on white symbol fields displayed on a black sign background.

The illustration shows the result of the testing of the Ticket Purchase symbol.

The distances from which the Taxi symbol was legible were 10% greater, and for the Elevator symbol, 30% less.

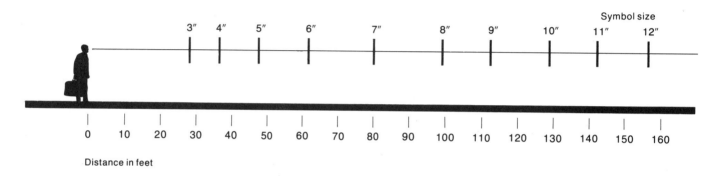

Distance in feet

One of the most important aspects of good signing is siting. The closer to one's natural line of vision, the better.

A useful rule of thumb is to avoid exceeding a 10 degree angle from the natural line of vision. This formula has value, primarily with regard to height, except in the case of a roadway or corridor type of condition where 'natural line of vision' can be reasonably defined.

If conditions require that the viewing angle exceeds 10 degrees, the size/distance relationship may have to be adjusted (for example, a sign at 15 feet above the floor level will probably have to be larger than the same sign at 8 feet to be as effective) or another smaller sign may have to be added for short-distance reading.

It must be pointed out that legibility varies greatly from one symbol to another, or from one type style to another, and that color relationships, lighting, spacing, and viewing angle may also affect legibility. We recommend pragmatic testing of symbols and lettering on-site, or in simulated on-site conditions.

If an attempt is made to 'equalize' symbols of unequal legibility in a signing system by varying their size, the result would be visually chaotic. We recommend that the legibility characteristics of the least legible symbols determine the size of all the symbols in a given system. This would provide a sense of order and adequate legibility throughout.

The intensity of internal lighting of symbols on translucent background material should be minimal to prevent loss of legibility due to 'halation,' the spreading of light.

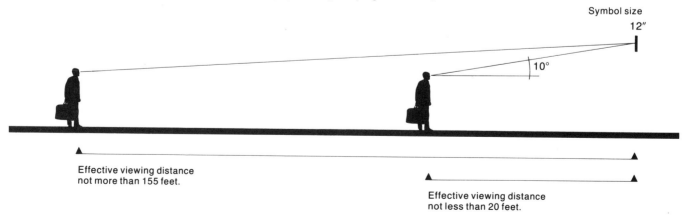

Effective viewing distance not more than 155 feet.

Effective viewing distance not less than 20 feet.

Determining Symbol/Letter Size Relationships

Using pragmatic testing, or the legibility diagrams, determine the required type and symbol size to ensure adequate legibility from the desired maximum viewing distance.

The symbols may exceed this size, if desired, but should not be less legible than the type unless unavoidable.

Lettering size should also be determined by testing, but a reasonably effective guide is to provide 1 inch of letter height for each 50 feet of viewing distance.

The size relationships shown in the following illustrations include 1/4:1, 1/3:1, and 2/5:1 and provide approximately equal legibility between the Helvetica Medium lettering used and the symbol. (This size relationship may not apply to other lettering styles.)

 1/4

 1/3

 2/5

Use of Grid

Within a given facility or system only one type style should be used, and a consistent 'vocabulary' of relationships be developed.

In order to aid in the development and application of an established 'vocabulary,' it is often good to use some kind of consistent 'grid' as a basis for the sign layouts. The grid used for the illustrations in these guidelines established certain key relationships; one symbol width between lettering and symbol, one half symbol width between arrow and symbol under most conditions, and one quarter symbol width between symbols.

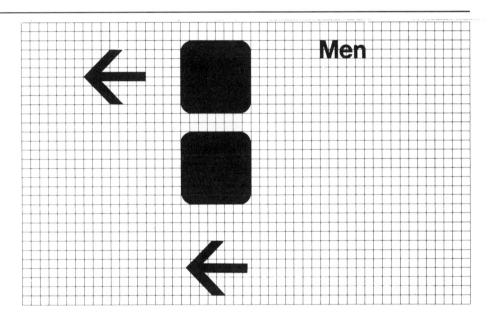

Lettering

In order to provide the freedom to respond meaningfully to varying architectural and cultural styles, no one lettering or type style must be used with the symbols.

Choice of a type style should take into account legibility and compatibility with the symbols and the environment. Lettering and word spacing affect the legibility and appearance of different lettering styles in varying ways at different distances. Color and lighting also affect spacing needs. Generally, the following 'rules of thumb' are useful:

White lettering on a dark background requires more letter spacing than does black on white.

Internally lighted letters may require greater letter spacing depending upon intensity of light.

Open letter spacing increases legibility from great distances. (Larger letters spaced tighter and occupying the same area may accomplish the same thing.)

Many type styles suffer aesthetically when open letter spacing is used.

Well executed optical letter spacing (either open or tight) is better than mechanical letter spacing.

Helvetica Medium (caps and lower case) was selected for illustrations in these guidelines because of its excellent legibility, compatibility with the symbols and aesthetic quality. Its extremely large 'x' height (the height

of lower case letters such as the x) also allows the use of both upper and lower case with relatively little size loss. The word shapes created by the ascending and descending letters aid in legibility.

Symbol Presentation

In order to ensure the legibility and recognition of the symbols, it is important that certain visual elements be kept consistent.

The drawing of the symbols and the proportional relationship of the figure (the drawing or symbolic device) to the symbol field (the square area with radius corners) must always be maintained.

The basic recommendation is to use black figures on a white field. Where design considerations require it, very dark or light colors, such as architectural bronze or natural stainless steel, may be used in lieu of black and white. To ensure good legibility, a strong dark/light contrast should be maintained.

The following examples illustrate application on a variety of backgrounds. From top to bottom:

Black sign background, white symbol field, black figure.

Grey (or other color) sign background. Be sure color is light enough to ensure that legibility of black lettering is not impaired. If dark sign background is desired, use white lettering. Test full size mock-up (in color) on-site, or in simulated on-site conditions.

White sign background. Outline field definition and black figure. This is the only condition in which the symbol outline should be delineated.

White sign background. Light grey (or light color) symbol field. Black figure.

Be sure color is light enough so that legibility of figure is not impaired. Never use outline and color field together.

Foreign Language Translations

Translations should be different from, but not subordinant to, the English messages. The same lettering style can be used for both, but then they should be presented in different colors as shown in the illustration, and

positioned in a manner that clearly separates them from the English. The color keying will make it easier to find the appropriate language.

Baggage Claim Livraison Bagages

A Suggested Directional Arrow

This directional arrow has been designed to complement the style and proportions of the recommended symbols.

To establish a relationship between arrow, symbol and lettering, the arrow can be thought of as being placed in a square module. The 8 directions it can point to are referenced within the square as shown in the example. The module is enlarged or reduced depending on sign type or grid being followed. Whatever size variations are established for a given sign system should remain constant throughout that system.

Note that the square grid is only for guidance in positioning the arrow. It is **not** intended that the square shape appear on the sign.

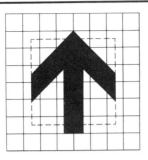  

Fabrication

It is essential that the symbols be accurately reproduced regardless of how they are made. Any variation in drawing or proportion will adversely affect their recognizability.

It is best to use the photographic methods, such as photo silk screening, or other printing techniques employing the use of an exact film replica of the original symbol in the making of printing plates or dies.

If photographic methods are not possible or practical, and hand cutting or painting must be employed,

full-sized photostats of the original symbols should be used as templates or guides, and very high standards of workmanship should be demanded of the sign maker.

Standardized red and green paint chips for certain symbol signs are included in this kit. These colors should be placed directly on paint samples for an accurate visual match.

If an offset printing ink is being used, rather than paint or silk screen ink, the closest colors in the Pantone Matching System are 032 (red) and 340 (green).

Examples

The illustrations on the following pages are presented primarily to demonstrate the versatility and effectiveness of the symbols in a variety of typical signing conditions.

To simplify this demonstration we have used one possible signing 'vocabulary'

throughout. Other styles and arrangements may be more desirable in response to specific architectural styles and conditions.

Location Signs

The illustrations below show two solutions to typical symbol sign problems. The first is a sign band and the second a hanging sign occupying less horizontal dimension.

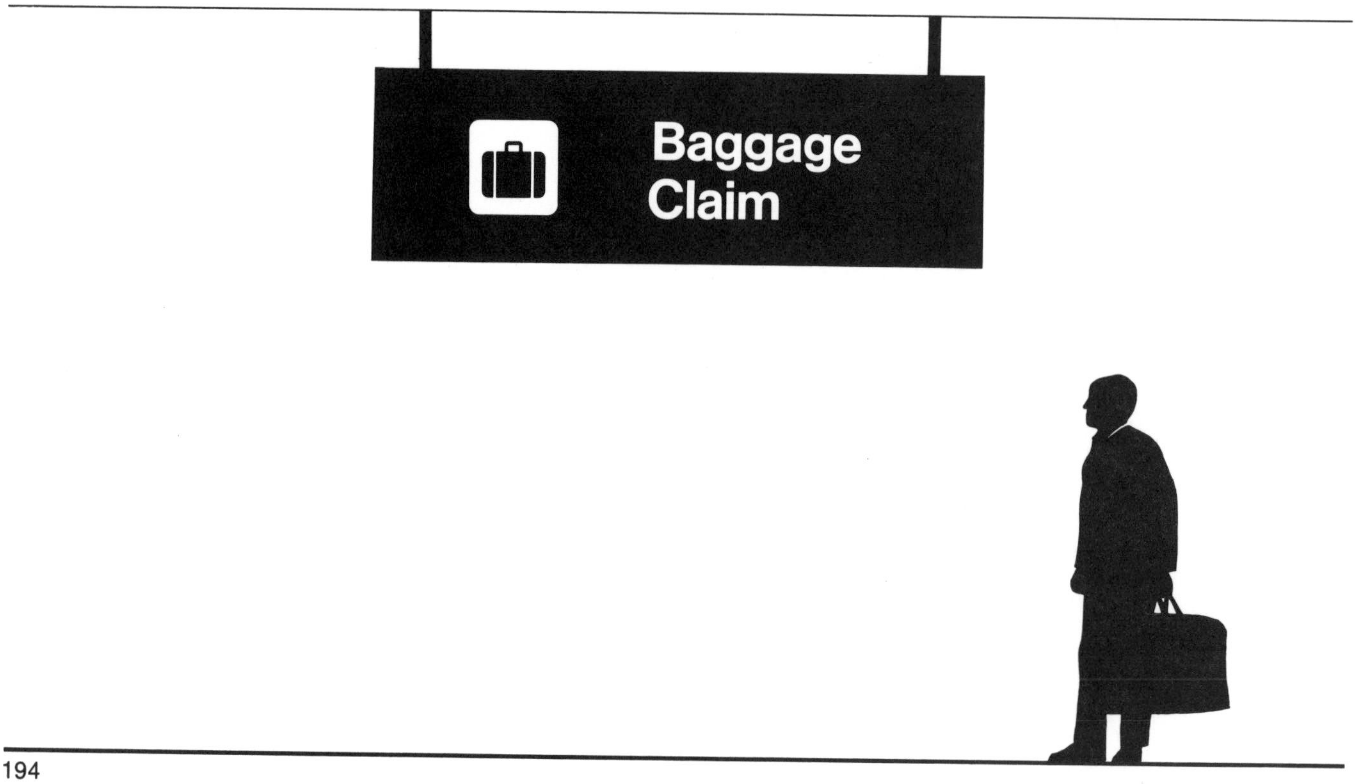

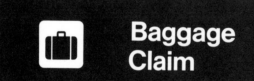

If the vertical dimension is restricted and the message must be visible from a great distance, the sign band variation shown below may be used. The illustration with the column displays a possible solution to a location sign with limited horizontal dimensions.

 **Baggage Claim**

Baggage
Claim

Uni-directional Signs

For uni-directional signs the arrow should be to the right when pointing to the right and to the left when pointing to the left. Note that the symbol separates the arrow from the lettering.

Ticket Purchase →

← **Ticket Purchase**

Multi-directional Signs

Where several directions are indicated
on one sign it is best to keep the arrow
in a constant position relative to the
symbols, regardless of arrow direction.

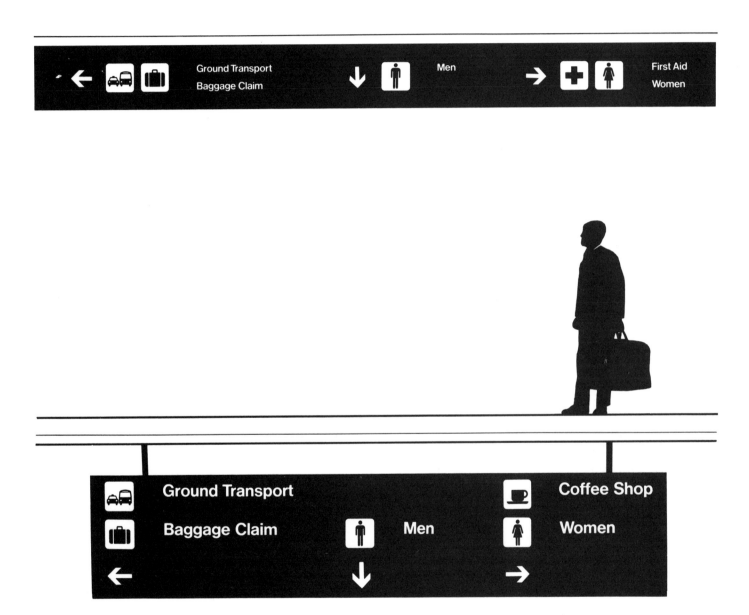

Door Signs

The examples below show a few of the
many ways that symbol signs can be
used to identify special rooms. Similar
signs may also be projected from the
wall for better visibility in 'corridor'
conditions.

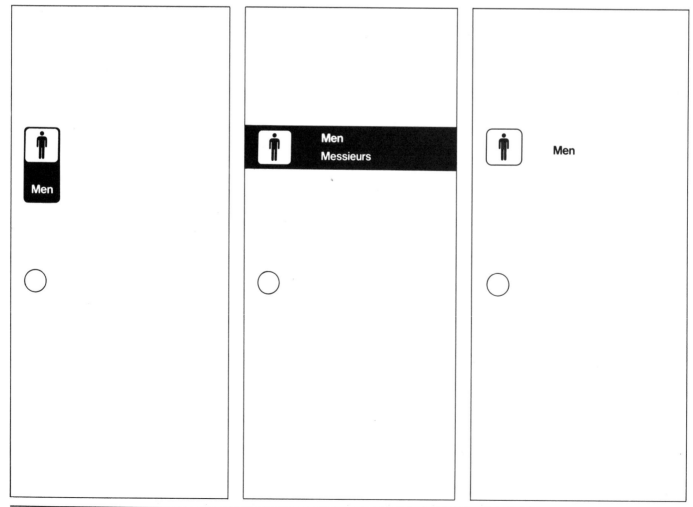

Curb Side Signs

Curb side signage should be carefully
sited to provide good sightlines from
cars, buses and trucks. The use of
reflective material for the symbol field
may be desirable if ambient light is not
adequate for night viewing.

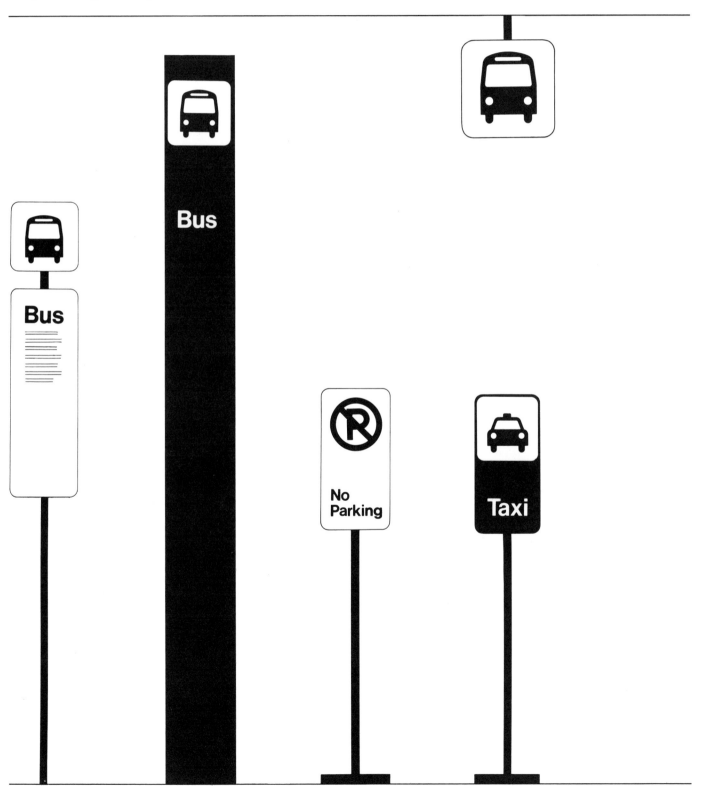

The illustrations demonstrate how a universally used symbol could help make the identification of the Fire Exit clear to a traveler who does not understand the local language. The words shown are among the many different ones now used in various parts of the world to identify this important location.

 EXIT

SORTIE

 AUSGANG

SALIDA

非常口

خروج

The symbol is basically a disc that is vertically bisected. It always appears green except when on a green field, in which case the symbol appears in white.

The illustrations show the various possible color combinations. They are not intended to be specific sign designs.

The color green has been selected because it is gradually becoming a universal standard for assistance or help. It is being established as the standard for all "way out" signs in Europe, and is also used in many states in this country, such as California, for all Exit signs. Green also, of course, commonly stands for "go" or "walk" on traffic signs.

As such, it seems to be a more appropriate choice than the red still being used for Exit identification in many parts of the country.

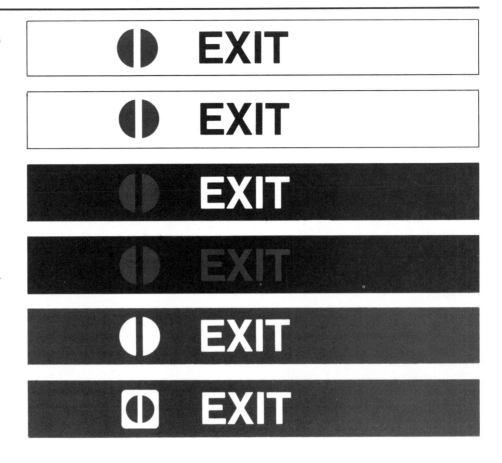

The proposed symbol could be combined with the appropriate word (e.g. EXIT) in a number of different ways. It would be best when incorporated as a basic part of the design of any new signs, but it could also be added as a decal where needed with existing signs.

There are currently in the U.S. so many different local regulations concerning the size, location and color of Exit signs that it is difficult to recommend specific relationships. Nevertheless the intent would be to use the word and symbol in combination until such time that the symbol became well enough established so that the word could be greatly reduced in size, and eventually eliminated.

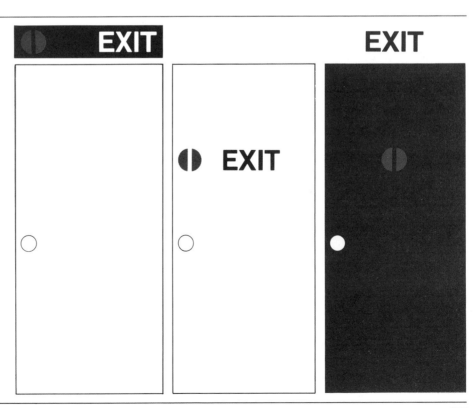

Terminology

Listed below is the suggested terminology for use on signs. The requirements of specific facilities will determine the exact terminology used.

Function	Terminology	Function	Terminology
Public Services		**Concessions**	
Telephone	Telephone	Car Rental	Car Rental
Mail	Mail		Rent-a-Car
	Post Office	Restaurant	Restaurant
Currency Exchange	Currency Exchange	Coffee Shop	Coffee Shop
	Bank		Snack Bar
Cashier	Cashier	Bar	Bar
First Aid	First Aid		Cocktails
Lost and Found	Lost and Found	Shops	Shops
Coat Check	Coat Check		News and Gifts
Baggage Lockers	Baggage Lockers	Barber Shop/Beauty	Barber Shop/Beauty
Escalator Up	Escalator	Salon	Salon
	Escalator Up	Barber Shop	Barber Shop
Escalator Down	Escalator	Beauty Salon	Beauty Salon
	Escalator Down		Hairdresser
Stairs Up	Stairs		
Stairs Down	Stairs		
Elevator	Elevator	**Processing Activities**	
Toilets, Men	Men		
Toilets, Women	Women	Ticket Purchase	Ticket Purchase
Toilets	Toilets	Baggage Check-in	Baggage Check-in
Nursery	Nursery	Baggage Claim	Baggage Claim
Drinking Fountain	Drinking Fountain	Customs	Customs
	Drinking Water	Immigration	Immigration
Waiting Room	Waiting Room	Departing Flights	Departing Flights
	Lounge	Arriving Flights	Passenger Pick-Up
Information	Information		
Hotel Information	Hotel Information		
Air Transportation	Air Transport	**Regulations**	
	Airport		
Heliport	Heliport	Smoking	Smoking
Taxi	Taxi	No Smoking	No Smoking
Bus	Bus	Parking	Parking
Ground Transportation	Ground Transport	No Parking	No Parking
Rail Transportation	Train(s)	No Dogs	No Dogs
Water Transportation	Water Transport		No Pets
	Ship(s)	No Entry	No Entry
	Pier(s)	Exit	Exit
		Fire Extinguisher	Fire Extinguisher
		Litter Disposal	Litter Disposal
			Trash

The concept of having a dark figure on a light background, contained within a symbol field of square shape with rounded corners, is still the basic format recommendation. The alternate formats shown were developed to provide flexibility in dealing with specific design problems. For example, the limited height of ceiling-hung signs may make distance visibility a critical problem. Taking the symbols out of a shape altogether allows one to make them larger within a given height, thus possibly increasing the distance from which they will be legible.

As another example, a map may be drawn in isometric form, where all the angles make it difficult to apply the square shape. In such a case the symbols alone, or in a round shape, may be preferable.

In no case, however, should the formats be mixed! Within any facility, or even system of facilities, one form should be established and used consistently throughout. Also, forms not shown here, such as ellipses, triangles, or irregular shapes, should **not** be used.

Finally note that the "reverse" concept (white symbol on dark field) can also be applied to the Figures Without a Symbol Field, and the Circular Symbol Field, even though it has not been demonstrated here.

Standard format

Figure without a symbol field

Figure in a reversed symbol field

Figure in circular symbol field

Shown here is the entire inventory of 50 symbols with the standard symbol field completely eliminated. Although the recommended method is to use the standard symbol field (square with rounded corners), there may be instances when the symbols must be adapted to a system where no symbol field appears at all. In this case, the figure by itself becomes the symbol.

Note that the elimination of the field also eliminates the recommended method for aligning and spacing the symbols. Ordinarily, the edges of the field provide guidelines for the distance between symbols and for a common baseline. In the case of the symbols below, visual spacing and placement must be carefully judged in order to avoid the appearance that the figures are "floating."

*The Toilets and Ground
Transportation symbols have been
enlarged to match the single Men,
Women, and Bus figures.

Shown here is the entire inventory of 50 symbols with a reversed standard symbol field. Although the recommended method is to use a black figure on a white standard symbol field (square with rounded corners), there may be instances where the symbols must be adapted to a system already using the reversed field, as shown below.

*Regulatory signs appear
 normally with red circle and
 slash.
**No Entry symbol appears red
 with white bar.
***Exit symbol always green.
****First Aid symbol always appears
 red in the U.S.

*

*

*

**

***

Shown here is the entire inventory of 50 symbols with a circular symbol field. Although the recommended method is to use a standard field (square with rounded corners), there may be instances, as with certain maps, where a circular field shape is more convenient.

To fit the figures into a circular field, appropriate proportional adjustments must be made.

*Note that the Barber Shop and
Beauty Salon symbols are the only
instances where the elements of the
"figure" must be rearranged to fit in
a circle.

Throughout the process of evaluation, selection, and design, decisions have been made subjectively by individuals and groups having wide experience in the problems of signage.

Beyond this method, however, it is quite difficult to objectively predetermine the effectiveness of any one symbol. Experience shows that constant repetition has more to do with effectiveness than does a difference in style of drawing or appropriateness of concept. The No Entry symbol is now understood in most Western countries because it has been widely used; it would be meaningless in an area where it had never been seen.

For the same reason, the results of survey tests taken at on-site locations have their limitations. Do most people recognize the handset as a symbol for telephone because it is a good symbol or because it has already been widely used? Would a different symbol for telephone, with equal exposure, have been even more effective? Can a symbol with very little exposure be expected to be well recognized?

With an understanding that such tests can provide only limited information, we do feel that use of the symbols in actual conditions can help point up any especially poor symbols or major defects in the overall system. Such testing should be carried out in a wide range of locations, at least some of which serve large numbers of foreign visitors.

We further recommend that any survey evaluations to be made at on-site locations be done professionally with the goals and methods clearly predetermined.

5

Appendix

BAA, British Airports Authority

  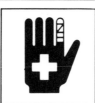  

CSS, Canadian National Signing System

D/FW, Dallas-Fort Worth International Airport

FA, Frankfurt Airport

IATA, International Air Transport Association

  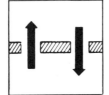  

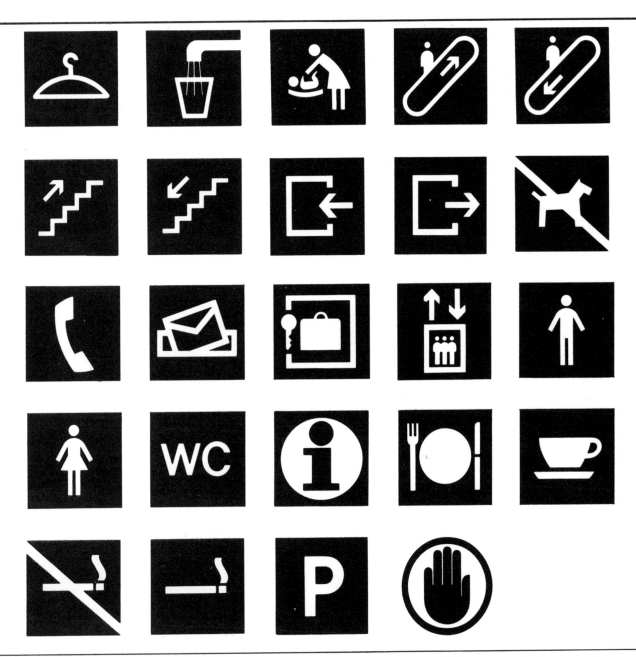

NPS, National Park Service

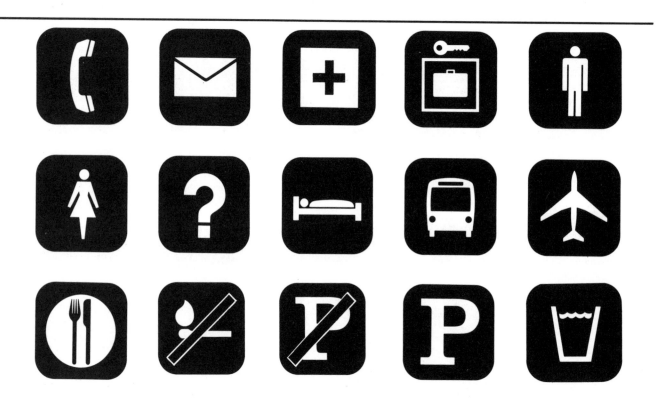

  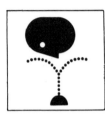 

   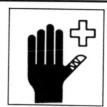 

O'72, Olympic Games, Munich 1972

   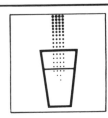 

O'76, Olympic Games, Montreal 1976

Port, Port Authority of New York and New Jersey

 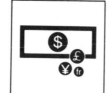 

Airport Buildings Sign Manual
1974
Airports and Construction Services
Airport Facilities Branch,
Ministry of Air Transport
Ottawa K1A ON8
Ontario, Canada

American Airlines Symbols
1973
Henry Dreyfuss Associates
888 Seventh Avenue
New York, N.Y. 10019

"Another Olympic Signing System"
1976
Print
Number XXX:111
pp. 31–35
RC Publications Inc.
355 Lexington Avenue
New York, N.Y. 10017

"Bildsymbole zur Erleichterung der Orientierung,
der Reisenden"
1965
International Union of Railways
14-16 Rue Jean Rey
Paris, France

"Canada's National Signing System"
1976
Print
Number XXX:111
pp. 36–39
RC Publications Inc.
355 Lexington Avenue
New York, N.Y. 10017

Crosby, Fletcher, Forbes
A Sign Systems Manual
1970
Praeger Publishers Inc.
111 Fourth Avenue
New York, N.Y. 10003

*Collection of Existing Pictographs Answering to
the Basic List of Informations*
1966
Aeroport de Paris
Paris, France

"Design Policy for Sapporo Winter
Olympic Games"
1972
Graphic Design
Number 45
pp.16-34
Kodansha Ltd.
2-12-21 Otowa
Bunkyo-ku
Tokyo, Japan

Dreyfuss, Henry
Symbol Sourcebook
1972
McGraw-Hill Book Publishers
330 West 42nd Street
New York, N.Y. 10036

Friluftsomradet
1972
Statens Naturvardsverk
Sweden

*International Signs to Facilitate
Passengers Using Airports*
1970
International Civil Aviation Organization
International Aviation Building
1080 University Street
Montreal 101,
Quebec, Canada

Katzumie Masaru
"Design Policy for the Munich Olympic Games 1972"
1972
Graphic Design
Number 47
Kodansha Ltd.
2-12-21 Otowa
Bunkyo-ku
Tokyo, Japan

Murakoshi Aisaku
"Visual Signs Connected with Traffic"
1971
Graphic Design
Number 43
Kodansha Ltd.
2-12-21 Otowa
Bunkyo-ku
Tokyo, Japan

"Picto'grafics"
1972
Architectural Graphics Inc.
Picto'grafics Systems Division
3 Koger Executive Center
Norfolk, Virginia 23502

Pictographs for Orientation at Airports
1968
German Airports Association
Arbeitsgemeinschaft Deutscher
Verkehrsflughafen
Geschaftsfuhrung
7023 Stuttgart,
Germany

Sapporo '72 Design Guide Sheets
1972
Japan

*Signing and Symbols in Signing for
Seattle-Tacoma International Airport*
1971
The Richardson Associates
215 Columbia Street
Seattle, Washington 98104

Signs of the Jet Age
1966
Arnold Thompson Associates
Airline Airport Technical Group of the Air
Transport Association
1709 New York Avenue NW
Washington, D.C. 20006

Spoorboekje '74/'75
1974
Nederlandse Spoorwegen,
Holland

*Standard Sign Manual
Expo 67*
1967
Canadian Corporation for the 1967 World
Exhibition

"Symbol Project for the Metro in Mexico",
1971
Graphic Design
Number 41
Kodansha Ltd.
2-12-21 Otawa
Bunkyo-ku
Tokyo, Japan

*U.S. Department of the Interior
National Park Service
Standard Sign Graphics Report*
1970
Chermayeff and Geismar Associates
830 Third Avenue
New York, N.Y. 10022